Indirect tax

(Finance Act 2014)

Tutorial

for assessments from January 2015

Michael Fardon
Jo Osborne

Published by Osborne Books Limited
Unit 1B Everoak Estate
Bromyard Road, Worcester WR2 5HP
Tel 01905 748071
Email books@osbornebooks.co.uk
Website www.osbornebooks.co.uk

Design by Laura Ingham

Printed by CPI Group (UK) Limited, Croydon, CRO 4YY, on environmentally friendly, acid-free paper from managed forests.

British Library Cataloguing in Publication Data
A catalogue record for this book is available from the British Library

ISBN 978 1909173 514

Contents

Acknowledgements

The publisher wishes to thank the following for their help with the reading and production of the book: Jon Moore and Cathy Turner. Thanks are also due to Alison Aplin for her technical editorial work and to Laura Ingham for her designs for this series.

The publisher is indebted to the Association of Accounting Technicians for its help and advice to our authors and editors during the preparation of this text.

Authors

Michael Fardon has extensive teaching experience of a wide range of banking, business and accountancy courses at Worcester College of Technology. He now specialises in writing business and financial texts and is General Editor at Osborne Books. He is also an educational consultant and has worked extensively in the areas of vocational business curriculum development.

Jo Osborne qualified as a Chartered Accountant with Ernst & Young in their London office. She then moved to Cable & Wireless where she spent two years in their internal audit department before moving into an investment appraisal role. Jo has taught AAT at Hillingdon College and until recently at Worcester College of Technology where she took on the role of AAT Coordinator.

Introduction

what this book covers

This book has been written specifically to cover the 'Indirect tax' Unit which is mandatory for the revised (2013) AAT Level 3 Diploma in Accounting.

The book contains a clear text with case studies, chapter summaries and key terms to help with revision. Each chapter has a wide range of activities, including many in the style of the computer-based assessments used by the AAT. In this edition all illustrations and calculations relating to standard rate VAT use the 20% rate.

AAT Reference material

This is made available to candidates during their Computer Based Assessments and is included in this book for assessments from 1 January 2015 until 31 December 2015. This reference material is produced by the AAT and reproduced here with their kind permission.

Osborne Workbooks

Osborne Workbooks contain practice material which helps students achieve success in their assessments. *Indirect tax (Finance Act 2014) Workbook* contains a number of paper-based 'fill in' practice exams in the style of the computer-based assessment. Please visit www.osbornebooks.co.uk for further details and access to our online shop.

1 Introduction to Value Added Tax

this chapter covers...

This chapter is an introduction to Value Added Tax (VAT) and the way in which businesses are affected by it.

It contains:

- a **definition** of Value Added Tax as a tax on sales and consumer expenditure
- the distinction between Value Added Tax as an **input tax** (on goods and services a business buys) and an **output tax** (on goods and services a business sells)
- an **overview** of the way in which a business is affected by VAT including the processes of:
    - entering transactions involving VAT into the accounting system of a business
    - extracting data from the accounts to work out the amount of VAT a business may have to pay, or reclaim
    - completion of the VAT Return
- details of the various **VAT rates**
- details of where to find **information** about VAT
- an explanation of the process by which a business becomes **VAT-registered** with HM Revenue & Customs (the Government body which regulates and collects VAT) describing:
    - who has to register
    - when they have to register and when they can deregister
- an explanation of how businesses are affected by the workings of **HM Revenue & Customs,** including inspections of the VAT records of a business

WHAT IS VALUE ADDED TAX?

a definition

Value Added Tax (VAT) is a tax on the sale of goods and services

VAT is therefore:

- a tax on **consumer expenditure** – it affects everyone in the UK purchasing most goods and services
- an **indirect tax** – consumers do not normally notice they are paying it, unlike income tax which is direct tax and very evident on a payslip

VAT is not only charged in the UK; many countries charge VAT (or a similar sales tax), and at varying rates.

VAT is an important source of revenue for the government which imposes it; the higher the rate, the more the government receives to finance its spending needs.

HM Revenue & Customs and VAT law

The Government body which regulates and collects VAT in the UK is **HM Revenue & Customs**, which also regulates other areas of taxation such as income tax and excise duties. The common abbreviation for this body is **HMRC**; we will be using this from time-to-time in this book.

VAT law in the European Union is governed by European Union Directives which are brought into effect in the UK by statute law: the Value Added Tax Act (1994), the annual Finance Acts, and other regulations issued by the government. Further regulation is provided by the **VAT Guide** (Notice 700) issued by HMRC. This Guide, together with supplementary notices, explains and interprets the VAT regulations. These are all available on the HM Revenue & Customs website – www.hmrc.gov.uk.

AN OVERVIEW OF VALUE ADDED TAX

Before explaining VAT in detail we will first provide an overview of the whole process of a business – a **supplier** of goods or services – which charges VAT and eventually pays the amount due to HMRC.

These processes start with registration.

registration for VAT

Businesses which supply goods and services will normally charge VAT, unless, of course, there is no VAT payable, for example, as in the case of the sale of food and young children's clothes. Businesses by law must **register** with HMRC for charging VAT if their annual sales reach a certain level.

There is a registration threshold set by the government each year, normally in the Budget. From April 2014 the threshold was set at £81,000.

If at the end of any month a supplier's total sales (turnover) for the previous twelve months exceeds this figure, or is likely to exceed this figure during the next 30 days, that supplier must by law register with HM Revenue & Customs to become what is known as a **taxable person**.

The effect of this registration means that the supplier (taxable person):

- must charge VAT on chargeable supplies (ie goods and services)
  - this is known as **output tax**
- can reclaim VAT paid on most business supplies received
  - this is known as **input tax**

As most businesses are run to make a profit – ie more money will be received from sales than is spent on supplies – most businesses will charge more VAT (output tax) than they pay (input tax). The difference between these two must be paid to HMRC, the figure is calculated and input online on a form known as the **VAT Return** (see page 7).

VAT – a tax on the final consumer

It is important to note at this stage that VAT is a tax which is finally paid by the **final consumer** of the goods.

If a member of the public buys a computer for £720 and the VAT rate is, for example, 20%, the amount paid includes VAT of £120 (ie 20% of £600). The buyer stands the cost of the VAT, but the VAT is actually paid to HM Revenue & Customs by all the businesses involved in the manufacturing and selling process.

This is illustrated by the diagram on the opposite page. You will see that the right hand column shows the amount of VAT paid to HM Revenue & Customs at each stage in the process. The supplier of raw materials, the manufacturer and the shop all pay over to HM Revenue & Customs the difference between VAT on sales (outputs) and VAT on purchases (inputs), but this amount is collected from the next person in the process. It is the **consumer** who pays the VAT bill at the end of the day. This VAT is paid to the shop, but as you can see from the diagram, the tax is paid in various stages to HM Revenue & Customs.

collection and payment of Value Added Tax to HMRC

manufacture and sale of a computer

VAT payments to HM Revenue & Customs

supplier of materials

- keeps £200
- pays £40 to HM Revenue & Customs

sells materials for £200 plus £40 VAT = £240

£40

plus

manufacturer

- keeps £440
- pays £48 to HM Revenue & Customs (difference between £88 collected and £40 paid to supplier of materials)

adds on margin and sells computer for £440 plus £88 VAT = £528

£48

plus

shop

- keeps £600
- pays £32 to HM Revenue & Customs (difference between £120 collected and £88 paid to manufacturer)

adds on margin and sells computer for £600 plus £120 VAT = £720

£32

plus

final consumer

- pays nothing **directly** to HM Revenue & Customs (the £120 has all been paid to the shop)

buys computer for £600 plus £120 VAT = £720

£0

equals

£120

the flow of VAT data – financial transactions

Later in this book (Chapters 4 and 5) we will describe in detail how VAT data from the accounting system of a business is used to provide the figures for entry on the VAT Return.

In this chapter we are taking an overview of how the process works, starting with financial transactions and finishing with the sending of the VAT Return and payment to HM Revenue & Customs.

Study the diagram below and read the text that follows.

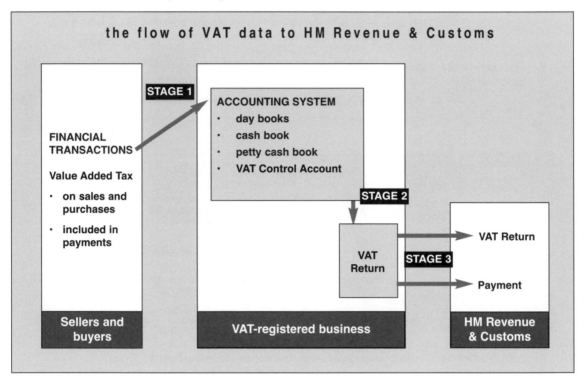

Stage 1 – financial transactions to accounts

The first stage is the transfer of VAT information from the documents which are generated by financial transactions into the accounting system of the business. The process is as follows:

■ The VAT figures on invoices and credit notes and the VAT included in payments are transferred to the day books, cash book and petty cash book in the accounting system of the business.

■ The VAT totals from these accounting records are then transferred to a **VAT control account** in the ledger accounts; this account forms a collection point for these totals and other VAT figures which are transferred from the accounts.

Stage 2 – accounts to VAT Return

- Figures from the **VAT control account** and other accounts recording sales (outputs) and purchases (inputs) are then transferred to the VAT Return (see below).

  Any sales or purchases made within the EC are also included, together with the VAT totals which relate to these. The VAT Return works out the total amount owing to (or owed by) HMRC by deducting input VAT from output VAT.

Stage 3 – VAT Return to HM Revenue & Customs

- The final stage in the process is the submission of the VAT Return by the due date (usually every three months) to HM Revenue & Customs. This form is completed online and sent electronically to HMRC.

- Payment of VAT due to HMRC will also be made by the due date, and electronically in the great majority of cases.

VAT due in this period on **sales** and other outputs (Box 1):* [   ]
⑦

VAT due in this period on **acquisitions** from other **EC Member**
States (Box 2):* [   ]
⑦

Total VAT due **(the sum of boxes 1 and 2)** (Box 3):   **Calculated value**

VAT reclaimed in this period on **purchases** and other inputs,*
(including acquisitions from the EC) (Box 4): [   ]
⑦

Net VAT to be paid to HM Revenue & Customs or reclaimed by   **Calculated value**
you **(Difference between boxes 3 and 4)** (Box 5):

Total value of **sales** and all other outputs excluding any VAT.*
Include your box 8 figure (Box 6): [   ]
⑦
Whole pounds only

Total value of **purchases** and all other inputs excluding any*
VAT. **Include your box 9 figure** (Box 7): [   ]
⑦
Whole pounds only

Total value of all **supplies** of goods and related costs, excluding*
any VAT, to other **EC Member States** (Box 8): [   ]
⑦
Whole pounds only

Total value of all **acquisitions** of goods and related costs,*
excluding any VAT, from other **EC Member States** (Box 9): [   ]
⑦
Whole pounds only

If you want to save a draft copy of this return, please click the 'Save draft return' button below,
alternatively click 'Next' to continue to submit your VAT return.

(Back)   (Save draft return)   (Next)

---

an online VAT Return

RATES OF VAT

There are currently three rates of VAT in the UK:

- standard rate   20%
- reduced rate (eg on domestic fuel or power)   5%
- zero rate (eg on most food)   0%

There are also goods and services which are outside the scope of VAT and on which no VAT is charged, eg motorway tolls and charitable donations.

Zero-rated supplies are not the same as exempt supplies, although the result is the same – no VAT is charged. This is explained below.

zero-rated supplies

Zero-rated supplies are goods and services taxed at 0%. This may sound odd, but all it means is that the supplies are taxable, but the Government has decided that no tax should be charged, normally because the goods are an essential part of household spending and to tax them would place a burden on the less well-off. Examples of zero-rated supplies are:

- most food bought in shops, but not in restaurants
- young children's clothes and shoes
- transport – eg bus and train fares
- newspapers, magazines and books

An important point here is that businesses that sell zero-rated goods can reclaim the VAT charged (the input tax) on supplies that they have bought. For example, there was no VAT charged on this book, but the publisher was able to reclaim the VAT paid on the costs of the publishing process and the marketing costs. The situation with exempt supplies is quite different.

exempt supplies

Whereas zero-rated supplies are chargeable – at 0% – exempt supplies are not chargeable at all. Also, a supplier who supplies only VAT-exempt goods or services cannot reclaim any input VAT on purchases. Examples of supplies that are mostly exempt include:

- health and dental care
- education and training
- betting and gambling
- burials and cremations

You should read the 'VAT Guide' which illustrates these points further. This is available on www.hmrc.gov.uk as Notice 700.

SOURCES OF INFORMATION FOR VAT

The administration of VAT is a very complex process, and business organisations (and students of VAT) need regular easy access to accurate information and advice.

Some of this information changes frequently, which poses an extra challenge. VAT rates may vary and each Government Budget inevitably brings in further changes and new measures. The previous page, for example, gives the percentage rates of VAT which were correct when this book went to press. You are advised to check that these are still current when you read this.

VAT information online

Nowadays online information about individual areas of VAT is made readily available through search engines such as Google. Two useful sites are:

■ **www.hmrc.gov.uk**

This is the site of HM Revenue & Customs which has a direct link to a VAT section on its home page. The principle document produced by HMRC is the VAT Guide (Notice 700). This is an immense document which has many links to supplementary documents and notices, but it is reasonably well indexed and has search boxes which will enable you to find what you are looking for.

■ **www.businesslink.gov.uk**

This body has been set up by the Government to provide information and support to businesses to help them comply with regulations and improve their performance. The website is a mine of information and contains a useful section on VAT.

There is also updating information – which includes changes in VAT – produced on the websites of the major accounting firms after each Budget.

VAT information – paper-based sources

The problem with paper-based resources is that you face the danger that they may be out-of-date by the time that you read them. Always check the publication date carefully. Useful sources of reference material include:

■ the HMRC VAT Guide in paper format

■ reference manuals and CDs subscribed to by accounting firms (if you have access to them) - for example, the Gee VAT Factbook

■ tax updates published by firms of accountants in booklet form

But remember to check the publication date!

VAT information – other sources

Another way that you can keep up-to-date with changes in VAT practices is to attend relevant Continuing Professional Development (CPD) updates. These will be organised and run by the professional accounting bodies that have specialist staff with detailed up-to-date knowledge on VAT matters. In addition to this, obtaining relevant CPD meeting with other accounting professionals and reading relevant articles in journals and magazines will help to ensure you have the most current VAT knowledge available.

REGISTRATION FOR VAT

the need to register – the regulations

A person in business selling goods and services on which VAT is chargeable must apply to HM Revenue & Customs to become VAT-registered. This is required:

- when the value of the taxable supplies (the **taxable turnover**) over a twelve month period has exceeded a registration limit set annually by the Government (£81,000 from April 2014) – the person must apply within 30 days of the end of the 12 months

- when the value of the taxable supplies (the annual taxable turnover) is likely during the next 30 days to exceed the registration limit

In short, a person must apply to the local VAT Office to register (within 30 days) if taxable supplies have exceeded, or are likely to exceed the annual limit. If this registration is not carried out within the 30 day time limit the person can be fined – the reason being that the supplier will be failing to collect tax due to HM Revenue & Customs.

Suppliers of zero-rated goods and services are included in these regulations, although they may apply for exemption from registration. It is unlikely that they will do so, however, because then they will lose the right to reclaim any VAT on goods and services they have purchased, and will be out of pocket!

It is critical that a person should register for VAT if the supplies are chargeable. There have been cases of profitable businesses which have not registered and have been 'discovered' by HM Revenue & Customs after a period of years: they have had to pay from their own resources all the VAT they should have charged and have been bankrupted in the process.

who should register?

In the eyes of the HMRC, an individual or organisation that is in business is known as a **taxable person** and should register for VAT if sales are over the annual threshold. This term 'person' is fairly wide ranging and includes:

- sole proprietors (ie individuals)
- partnerships (ie groups of individuals)
- limited companies or groups of companies
- clubs and associations
- charities
- any other organisation or group of people acting together under a particular name, for example an educational establishment

taking over a going concern

If you intend to take over a business that is already a going concern, it may already be registered for VAT. However you may need to register at the date you buy the business. The VAT rules for the purchase of a business as a going concern are complex. Basically if the total of your turnover and the turnover of the business you are taking over exceeds the VAT registration threshold then you must be registered for VAT from the day that the business is transferred to you.

exception from registration

The turnover of a business may exceed the VAT threshold but this may only be temporary, for example due to a significant one-off sale. Provided the business can provide evidence and explain why the value of its taxable supplies will not go over the deregistration threshold in the next 12 months it can apply to HMRC not to register for VAT.

Note: if turnover goes over the VAT limit temporarily and the business does not notify HMRC within 30 days, it will not be able to request an exception. Instead it will have to register and then apply to be de-registered.

a business or not a business?

Only a **business** can register for VAT and become a 'taxable person'. HMRC defines a 'business' as a continuing activity involving getting paid for providing goods or services.

A 'taxable person' is in business when he or she:

- earns an income by carrying out a trade, vocation or profession
- provides membership benefits as a club or association in return for a subscription
- carries out activities as a charity or other non-profit making body

In order to qualify for being a business the person must carry out these activities regularly and over a period of time. This would exclude hobbies and other private activities, even if they involve buying and selling. If you occasionally sold your belongings on a website such as E-bay, for example, or went in for the occasional car-boot sale, that would not be a business activity. If, however, you did this on a regular and frequent basis to make money, you would be classed as a business and would need to become VAT-registered, if your taxable turnover reached the VAT threshold.

non-registered businesses

Businesses that have a turnover below the annual limit do not have to register for VAT or charge VAT. This can be useful for a business owner, for example, because he or she can in effect become more competitive and does not have to charge VAT to the consumer for goods and services, although the trader cannot reclaim VAT paid on supplies he or she has bought. Many small traders such as plumbers, electricians and gardeners who sell their skills may therefore be able to benefit by not having to register for VAT.

This is not the same as the practice adopted by some dishonest VAT-registered businesses saying to their customers "If you pay me cash in hand you won't have to pay the VAT". This is illegal and an attempt to defraud HM Revenue & Customs (and eventually the taxpayer!) of the VAT due.

voluntary registration

This situation is quite different from non-registration.

A supplier whose taxable turnover falls below the annual limit may **voluntarily register** for VAT, even if he or she does not need to do so. This is normally because he or she will benefit from claiming back input tax on purchases, eg if the business sells zero-rated goods, such as books or childrens clothes. This results in extra cash being received by the supplier – this would not be received if the business was not VAT-registered.

Another advantage of voluntary registration is that it may be possible to reclaim VAT on purchases of goods and capital assets held on the effective date of registration. There is normally a time limit of three years for goods, and six months for services.

Remember that the main point of voluntary registration is for a business to take advantage when the goods or services supplied are **zero-rated**. A business that supplies only **VAT-exempt** goods or services cannot reclaim any input VAT on purchases.

Voluntary registration carries with it all the responsibilities of VAT registration: a business must keep all the required VAT records and submit a VAT Return on the due dates.

deregistration

If a business finds that annual turnover falls – or is likely to fall – below a certain limit (£79,000 from April 2014) that business can apply to HM Revenue & Customs and **deregister**, if it seems advantageous to do so. This can be done by completing a paper-based form, or deregistering online. This might happen, for example, if a sole trader is running down the business before retirement.

practicalities of registration

- registration can be carried out online through www.hmrc.gov.uk or by downloading and completing the necessary forms
- when a person has been registered for VAT, a registration certificate will be issued giving full details of registration, including the **VAT number** which must be quoted on VAT invoices
- VAT paid by the person on expenses in setting up the business may normally be reclaimed
- VAT must be charged on sales as soon as registration takes place

REGULATION BY HM REVENUE & CUSTOMS

We have already seen in the last few pages that HM Revenue & Customs is the official body with which businesses must register for VAT purposes. As noted earlier in this chapter, HM Revenue & Customs acts as regulator and enforcer for all matters connected with VAT; this is in addition to its responsibilities for other types of taxation and for excise duties. The requirements of HMRC are therefore legal requirements.

All this affects businesses in a number of different areas, including:

- registration (which we have already explained on pages 10-12)
- the submission of VAT Returns and other documentation
- the keeping of VAT records
- inspecting the records of registered businesses

We will deal with the last three of these in turn.

Returns to HM Revenue & Customs

As we will see in Chapter 5, the **VAT Return**, which sets out the calculations for the amount of VAT that will need to be paid to (or claimed from) the HMRC is the main online form that businesses must complete. It must be accurate and it must be submitted on time.

Another required document is the **EC Sales List**. This is completed by UK VAT-registered businesses which supply VAT-rated goods or services to traders registered for VAT in other EC Member States. The list (see page 50 for an example) sets out details of the EC supplies and is used to control the taxation on movements of goods within the EC.

business records to be kept

HM Revenue & Customs requires that all VAT-registered businesses should maintain a full set of accurate business records. These should provide evidence that the VAT charged and claimed on the VAT Return is correct.

The records that should be maintained include:
- annual accounts, including the income statement
- the VAT control account and any associated working papers
- ledger accounts, cash book, petty cash book, sales and purchases day books
- sales invoices (copies) and purchase invoices
- bank statements and paying-in slips
- documentation relating to any EC sales and acquisitions, and imports and exports to non-EC countries
- any related correspondence and contracts
- a valid VAT certificate of registration

retention period for the business records

HM Revenue & Customs recommends that business keep their financial records for at least six years. Normal business practice suggests that the retention period should be six years plus the current year. The reason for this requirement is that HMRC regularly send VAT inspectors to businesses to check through these records and ensure that:
- the records are accurate and complete
- the business is complying with all the VAT regulations
- the business is paying (or claiming for) the correct amount of VAT

VAT inspectors

There is often a picture given of a VAT inspection being a nerve-racking and unwelcome experience. This will only be the case if the business has something to hide and has been engaged in avoiding the payment of VAT due to the Government. Normally a visit can be expected approximately every five years, although the interval may depend on how reliable the business has proved to be in the past.

VAT inspectors check businesses to make sure that their VAT records are up-to-date. They also check that amounts paid to (or claimed from) the Government through HM Revenue & Customs are correctly calculated.

They will examine the VAT records and ask questions of the business owner, or the person responsible for the VAT records. A visit may take from a couple of hours to several days – it all depends on the nature of the business.

When the inspection has been completed, the VAT officer will review with the business the work carried out during the visit and explain any areas of concern that they have identified, discuss them with the business owner (or manager) and agree any future action needed. If any adjustment is needed to be made to the amount of VAT payable, it will also be discussed and the amount of overpayment or underpayment agreed.

VAT inspections are not necessarily bad news: often the inspectors will give advice and suggest ways of improving the accuracy and efficiency of the accounting function of the business. However if there is a major fraud taking place, they will soon identify the problem and take action to recover the underpaid VAT.

In short, the best policy for a business in relation to HMRC requirements is to:

- keep the business records, books of accounts and all payments up-to-date
- always provide HMRC with the information they request within the specified time
- if in doubt, contact HMRC about any issues over which the business needs guidance and advice – HMRC can be contacted via a helpline or by letter to the local VAT Office
- get **written** confirmation from HMRC about issues on which doubt may arise as to the correct treatment for VAT

Chapter Summary

- Value Added Tax (VAT) is a tax on sales of goods and services and therefore a tax on consumer expenditure.

- VAT is administered and regulated by HM Revenue & Customs (HMRC) which is a Government body which has responsibility for a wide range of taxes.

- VAT is paid by the final consumer but is collected and paid to HM Revenue & Customs by the businesses involved in the selling and manufacturing processes.

- A VAT-registered person must pay to HM Revenue & Customs the VAT charged on sales (output tax) less tax on purchases (input tax). If input tax exceeds output tax a refund is due. The payment or refund is calculated on the regular VAT Return (VAT 100).

- VAT is charged at different rates: standard (most supplies), reduced (eg on domestic fuel) and zero (eg on food). These (except for zero rate) may be changed from time-to-time. Goods and services that are VAT-exempt are not liable to VAT at all.

- The most up-to-date and comprehensive source of information about VAT is to be found online. The website www.hmrc.gov.uk is the best source. Paper-based sources must be checked to see that they are in-date.

- A person must register for VAT if annual sales liable to VAT exceed (or are likely to exceed within 30 days) an annual threshold. That 'taxable person' must be in business and can be an individual, partnership, limited company, club, association or charity which charges for its goods or services.

- A business with annual sales below the VAT threshold may voluntarily register if there is an advantage gained from doing so, for example selling zero-rated goods (no VAT charged) and being able to claim back input VAT paid on expenses related to those sales.

- If the annual sales of a VAT-registered business fall below an annual threshold (normally slightly below the registration limit), that business can apply to deregister.

- A business must submit accurate returns by the due date to HM Revenue & Customs. These include the VAT Return, and for businesses that sell to the EU, Sales Lists. These are normally submitted online.

- As part of its regulatory role, HM Revenue & Customs will regularly inspect VAT-registered businesses, partly to ensure that they are paying the correct amount of VAT and also to provide help and advice where it is needed.

Key Terms	**Value Added Tax**	a tax imposed on the sale of goods and services
	indirect tax	a tax which is imposed indirectly on consumers by taxing their spending
	HM Revenue & Customs	the Government body which regulates and administers the collection of tax – including VAT
	VAT Guide 700	an online guide published by HMRC which explains the workings of VAT
	taxable person	a supplier who has been registered for VAT – the taxable person can be a sole trader, a partnership, a limited company, a group of companies, a club or association, or a charity
	output tax	VAT on sales of goods and services
	input tax	VAT on purchases of goods and services
	VAT 100	the HM Revenue & Customs VAT Return, which calculates VAT to be paid or refunded by deducting input tax from output tax
	standard rate	the basic percentage rate at which VAT is charged on most goods and services
	reduced rate	a reduced rate allowed for socially beneficial items such as domestic fuel
	zero-rated supplies	supplies which are liable to VAT, but at zero per cent
	exempt supplies	supplies which are not liable to VAT at all
	VAT registration	the formal procedure by which a business registers with HM Revenue & Customs and will then charge VAT and account for VAT due to HMRC
	VAT threshold	an amount set by HMRC for annual sales of a business, above which the business must register for VAT
	voluntary registration	VAT registration of a business whose annual turnover is below the VAT threshold
	deregistration	where the annual sales of a VAT-registered business falls below a certain threshold and the business applies to HMRC to cease charging VAT and being VAT-registered
	VAT inspection	regular visit to a business by HMRC VAT officers who check that VAT is being charged correctly

Activities

1.1 VAT charged by a supplier on a sales invoice is known as:

(a)   input tax

(b)   output tax

(c)   consumer tax

(d)   supplier tax

Which **ONE** of these options is correct?

1.2 The form summarising total input tax and output tax which a business must regularly send to HM Revenue & Customs is known as:

(a)   a VAT Return

(b)   a Sales List

(c)   a Registration return

(d)   a VAT control account

Which **ONE** of these options is correct?

1.3 The amount of VAT due to HM Revenue & Customs can be calculated as follows:

(a)   output tax plus input tax

(b)   output tax minus input tax

(c)   output tax divided by input tax

(d)   output tax multiplied by the VAT rate

Which **ONE** of these options is correct?

1.4 A purchase invoice with VAT for taxable supplies is being processed by the VAT-registered business that receives it. What will be the effect on the amount of VAT due to be paid to HM Revenue & Customs by this business?

(a)   it will decrease the amount due to be paid

(b)   it will increase the amount due to be paid

(c)   it will have no effect at all

(d)   it depends on the annual sales threshold set for VAT registration

Which **ONE** of these options is correct?

1.5 A VAT-registered business receives a credit note from a supplier. The document shows a VAT amount of £6.70. What effect will this have on the amount of VAT due to HM Revenue & Customs by this business?

(a) it will increase by £6.70 multiplied by the VAT rate

(b) it will decrease by £6.70, which is the VAT amount on the credit note

(c) it will stay the same because the input VAT will cancel out the output VAT

(d) it will increase by £6.70, which is the VAT amount on the credit note

Which **ONE** of these options is correct?

1.6 A customer buys goods costing £180 from a shop and VAT of £30 is included in this amount. This will be eventually be paid to HM Revenue & Customs:

(a) by the customer

(b) by the customer and the shop

(c) by the manufacturer and the supplier of the materials for the product

(d) by the manufacturer and the supplier of the materials for the product and the shop

Which **ONE** of these options is correct?

1.7 A zero rate of VAT appearing on an invoice for goods supplied means that:

(a) the supplier is not registered for VAT

(b) the goods are VAT-exempt

(c) the goods are chargeable but the rate is zero per cent

(d) the purchaser does not have to pay the VAT amount that is shown

Which **ONE** of these options is correct?

1.8 According to HM Revenue & Customs regulations a trader must register for VAT if:

(a) the value of her taxable supplies over the last six months has exceeded the registration threshold set by HM Revenue & Customs

(b) the value of her taxable supplies over the last twelve months has exceeded the registration threshold set by HM Revenue & Customs

(c) the estimated value of her taxable supplies over the next twelve months is likely to exceed the registration threshold set by HM Revenue & Customs

(d) the estimated value of her taxable supplies over the next six months is likely to exceed the registration threshold set by HM Revenue & Customs

Which **ONE** of these options is correct?

1.9   The following person is entitled to register for VAT:

(a)   an individual who sets up a shop in the town where she lives

(b)   an individual who occasionally sells his possessions on an online auction site

(c)   an individual who advertises in the local paper the contents of a house he has inherited

(d)   an individual who is an amateur pilot and sometimes charges people for rides in her plane

Which **ONE** of these options is correct?

1.10   A trader might choose voluntary registration for VAT because:

(a)   the total of his taxable supplies over the last twelve months has exceeded the registration threshold

(b)   he would be able to deregister in the future, even if his annual sales exceeded the annual threshold

(c)   his business would benefit because it would be able to reclaim input VAT on VAT-exempt invoices

(d)   his business would benefit because it would be able to reclaim input VAT on standard-rated invoices

Which **ONE** of these options is correct?

1.11   HM Revenue & Customs states that VAT records should be kept by a business for a minimum of:

(a)   six months

(b)   six years

(c)   twelve months

(d)   twelve years

Which **ONE** of these options is correct?

1.12   HM Revenue & Customs regularly send their officers to inspect all businesses which:

(a)   have applied for VAT registration

(b)   have applied for voluntary registration

(c)   are already VAT-registered and have an annual sales turnover of £1 million or more

(d)   are already VAT-registered, to ensure they are complying with the VAT regulations

Which **ONE** of these options is correct?

for your notes

2 VAT and business documents

this chapter covers...

The last chapter dealt with theoretical aspects of VAT. In this chapter we turn to the 'nuts and bolts' of how VAT works in practice. This chapter explains how VAT should be shown on a variety of business documents and also how a number of common VAT calculations are carried out.

The documents covered include:

- *standard VAT invoices used within the UK and 'less detailed' VAT invoices*
- *invoices for zero-rated and VAT-exempt supplies of goods and services*
- *pro-forma invoices*
- *VAT receipts*
- *EU customer invoices – used when selling to states within the European Union*

VAT calculations are needed from time-to-time in business and in this chapter we show how a number of calculations are carried out, including calculations for:

- *VAT amounts using a variety of rates and using the 'rounding' rule*
- *VAT which is included in the total amount on a document such but not shown as a separate amount*
- *VAT when a settlement (prompt payment) discount is offered on an invoice*

You will also need to know about 'tax points' when dealing with documentation. A 'tax point' is the point at which a supply of goods or services is treated as taking place for the purposes of charging VAT. This is normally fairly obvious and will be the date on the invoice, but it can be complicated by issues such as payment being made in advance of the supply of goods or services or an invoice issued after the supply has been made. This chapter explains how 'basic' and 'actual' tax points are worked out.

VAT INVOICES

When a VAT-registered supplier sells goods or services, the supplier must give or send to the purchaser within 30 days a VAT invoice which contains information about the goods or services supplied. A copy of the invoice must be kept on file (paper or electronic) by the supplier.

A VAT-registered customer must receive a valid VAT invoice from the supplier in order to claim back the VAT paid on the purchase for their business. The requirements for the contents of a VAT invoice are laid down by HM Revenue & Customs and are set out in the **VAT Guide**.

A VAT invoice (see illustrations on the next two pages) must show:

- an invoice number which follows on from the number of the previous invoice
- the seller's name or trading name, and address
- the seller's VAT registration number
- the invoice date
- the time of supply (also known as the tax point) if this is different from the invoice date
- the customer's name or trading name, and address
- a description of the goods or services supplied to the customer which enable the customer to identify what is being charged for

Most of the above details normally appear in the top half of the invoice (see next page). The one exception to this is the description of the goods or the service which appears lower down in the body of the invoice. This section should also contain, for each type of item sold:

- the unit price or rate (eg for a service), excluding VAT
- the quantity of goods (eg items) or the extent of the services (eg hours)
- the rate(s) of VAT that applies to what is being sold
- the total amount payable, excluding VAT
- the rate of any settlement (cash) discount
- the total amount of VAT charged

You will know from seeing different types of invoice that there are many different formats and other details, eg trade discounts, codes for products, customer accounts and terms and conditions. What HM Revenue & Customs are stating in the VAT Guide 700 is that the items listed above **must** be present on the invoice. Any other details and features may be added to the document to fit in with the requirements of the supplier.

Now study the invoices on the next two pages and see how they illustrate these requirements.

SALES INVOICE

Trend Designs

Unit 40 Elgar Estate, Broadfield, BR7 4ER
Tel 01908 765365　Fax 01908 7659507　Email lisa@trend.u-net.com
VAT Reg GB 0745 4172 20

invoice to

Crispins Fashion Store 34 The Arcade Broadfield BR1 4GH	

invoice no	787906
account	3993
your reference	1956
date/tax point	21 04 20-5

deliver to

as above

details	quantity	unit price	amount (excl VAT)	VAT rate %	VAT amount £
Schwarz 'T' shirts (black)	20	5.50	110.00	20	22.00
Snugtight leggings (black)	15	12.50	187.50	20	37.50

terms
Net monthly
Carriage paid
E & OE

Total (excl VAT)	297.50
VAT	59.50
TOTAL	357.00

This invoice has been issued by a supplier of fashion clothes, Trend Designs, to Crispins Fashion Store on 21 April (the tax point). Note that all the requirements of a VAT invoice are met: both items sold are charged at the standard rate of tax and the unit price is shown.

The VAT total of £59.50 will be recorded as output tax for Trend Designs and as input tax for Crispins Fashion Store. There is no cash discount offered and the buyer has to settle the full £357.00 a month after the invoice date.

SALES INVOICE

Paragon Printers

Partners: Edwin Parry, George Dragon
Unit 43 Elgar Estate, Broadfield, BR7 4ER
Tel 01908 765312 Fax 01908 7659551 Email Ed@paragon.u-net.com VAT Reg GB 0745 4672 71

invoice to

Prime Publicity Ltd 4 Friar Street Broadfield BR1 3RG	invoice no	787923
	account	3993
	your reference	47609
	date/tax point	07 05 20-5

deliver to

as above

details	unit price	amount (excl VAT)	VAT rate %	VAT amount £
Printing 2,000 A4 leaflets	189.00	189.00	zero	00.00
Supplying 2,000 C4 envelopes	75.00	75.00	20	15.00

terms
Net monthly
Carriage paid
E & OE

Total (excl VAT)	264.00
VAT	15.00
TOTAL	279.00

This invoice has been issued by a commercial printer, Paragon Printers, to Prime Publicity Limited on 7 May (the tax point) for goods delivered. Note that in this case there are two rates of VAT involved: printing is zero-rated and stationery is standard-rated. Where there are mixed VAT rates, as here, the two rates and VAT amounts must be quoted. The VAT total of £15.00 will be recorded as output tax for Paragon Printers and as input tax for Prime Publicity Ltd. There is no cash discount offered and the buyer has to settle the full £279.00 a month after the invoice date.

invoices for zero-rated and exempt supplies

If a business supplies goods and services which are zero-rated or exempt from VAT, the invoices issued must show this fact.

The zero-rated or exempt items should show clearly that there is no VAT payable and the value of the items must be shown separately.

situations where VAT invoices are not needed

There are a number of situations where VAT invoices are not compulsory:

■ where the buyer is not registered for VAT (although they must be given one if they ask)

■ where the seller is a retailer (although a customer can ask for one)

■ where the item is a free sample and normally subject to VAT

■ if the purchaser is on a **self-billing** system (ie the purchaser issues the invoice and sends it with the payment)

There are also situations where invoices may only show the VAT-inclusive amount (ie the total includes the VAT but does not state how much it is). These situations are:

■ where the transaction total is less than £250 (see below)

■ where the buyer, in agreement with the customer, issues an invoice in a modified format

simplified invoices – amounts under £250

If the amount charged for the supply is £250 or less (including VAT) a **simplified invoice** may be issued. This type of invoice must show:

■ the supplier's name, address and VAT registration number

■ the date of supply (tax point)

■ a description of the goods or services

■ the total charge payable for each item, **including** VAT

■ the VAT rate applicable to each item where the supply includes items at different VAT rates

If you receive one of these, to work out the amount of VAT in the VAT-inclusive price, you need to carry out a calculation, using the formula:

$$\frac{the\ total\ amount\ which\ includes\ VAT}{(100\% + VAT\%)} \quad x\ VAT\ \%$$

Another way of calculating the VAT in this situation is to multiply the whole amount by a 'VAT fraction' available from HM Revenue & Customs. This calculation is explained in full on page 31.

other types of invoice – pro-forma invoice

A further type of invoice is the **pro-forma invoice**. This is a document issued by a seller offering goods at a certain price and inviting the buyer to send a payment in return for which the goods will then be supplied and invoiced in the normal way.

This is a common arrangement when a seller receives an order from a new customer, but does not want to sell on credit – because there may well be a credit risk – and so needs payment up front.

A pro-forma invoice (see illustration below) may well look exactly like an invoice, but because it does not relate to a firm sale, **cannot be used as evidence to reclaim input tax**. Pro-forma invoices should be clearly marked 'THIS IS NOT A VAT INVOICE'. If a sale results from a pro-forma invoice, a separate invoice (a VAT invoice) should then be issued.

PRO-FORMA INVOICE

SPICER STATIONERY
45 High Street
Mereford MR1 3TR
Tel 010903 443851
VAT Reg 422 8371 78

R M Electrical Ltd
56 High Street
Mereford MR5 8UH

13 May 20-5

Your ref Purchase Order 2934234

45 x A4 Box files (burgundy) @ £4.99 each	£224.55
VAT @ 20%	£44.91
TOTAL PAYABLE	£269.46

THIS IS NOT A VAT INVOICE.

A VAT invoice will be issued on receipt of the amount in full.

VAT receipt

Another document issued by VAT-registered businesses is the **VAT receipt**. You may have heard the question 'Do you want a VAT receipt?' when you fill up with fuel at a garage. Most people will probably say 'no,' but people claiming the cost of fuel as a business expense will say 'yes' because the business involved will want to reclaim the VAT on the fuel.

VAT receipts are not always issued by VAT-registered retailers, but a customer has the right to demand one, particularly if businesses expenses are involved.

A valid VAT receipt needs to show the following details:

- the name, address and VAT registration number of the retailer
- items charged at different VAT rates listed separately

The VAT receipt shown below is for petrol and milk bought at a leading UK supermarket.

Study the format of the receipt and note the separate listing and coding (A and D) of the milk (zero-rated) and the petrol (standard-rated).

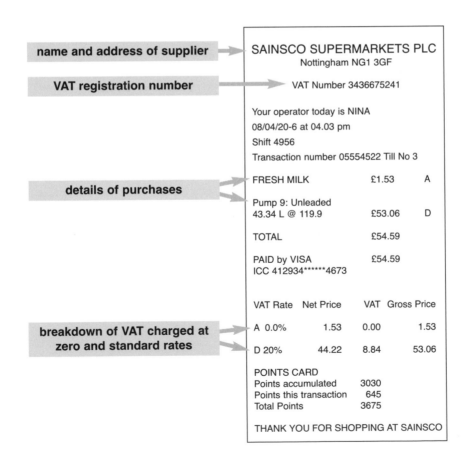

EU customer invoice

Businesses that sell goods and services within the European Union (EU) strictly speaking are not 'exporting' but sending 'dispatches'. This affects the rate the UK supplier has to charge VAT on supplies to a EU country. The situation is as follows:

■ if the buyer in the other EU state is **not registered** for VAT in that state, the UK supplier must charge **VAT at the normal UK rate** for the goods or services supplied

■ if the buyer in the other EU state **is registered** for VAT in that state, the UK supplier can usually **zero rate** the VAT charged (the ruling on VAT on services from business to business was amended in January 2010, bringing in certain exceptions to this zero-rating)

A business can only zero rate the VAT if the VAT registration number of the buyer (including the two letter country code) is shown on the **EU customer invoice**. The example below shows a dispatch of football boots to Bologna in Italy. The Italian VAT registration number – IT 294447382 – is highlighted in this example with a grey background.

INVOICE

ARMADILLO SPORTSWEAR

Unit 17 Manley Estate,
Hardy Road, Maxstone, Kent, MA4 5EW

Tel 01985 811314 Fax 01985 811376 Email sales@armadillo.co.uk

VAT Reg GB 0833 2672 10

---

invoice to

L A Mancini SRL
56 Via Gamberini Pietro
78423 Bologna
Italia

invoice no	73637
account	442
your reference	47609
date/tax point	09 04 20-3

description	quantity	price £	unit	total £
Robben football boots Ref 4555	45	50.00	each	2,250.00

Customer Intracommunity VAT number
IT 294447382

goods total £	2,250.00
VAT	00.00
TOTAL £	2,250.00

terms Net monthly, Carriage paid.
payment
Telegraphic transfer to Armadillo Sportswear, National Bank, Maxstone, 49 67 86, Account 84420363
IBAN: GB39HGCV2734646

VAT CALCULATIONS

In this section we illustrate some of the main calculation techniques that have to be carried out when preparing the VAT element of business documents such as invoices and receipts. These include:

- calculating VAT at different rates
- the rules for rounding of VAT amounts
- calculating the VAT content of a figure which contains VAT
- calculating VAT after trade discount and when a settlement (prompt payment) discount is offered on an invoice

calculating and rounding VAT

Calculation of VAT at various rates on invoices and receipts is a straightforward matter. More often than not it is all done electronically, either on a computer accounting package or on a shop checkout till.

When you are calculating VAT manually the problem of '**rounding**' arises. For example, if your calculator works out VAT due of £60.45674, what is the correct VAT amount in £s and pence?

HMRC allows businesses and other organisations issuing invoices to follow these procedures:

1   The **total** amount of VAT payable shown on an invoice or receipt can be **rounded down** to the nearest whole penny, so the total VAT due of £60.45674 would be shown as £60.45. This is different from the common method of rounding **up or down** to the nearest penny.

2   If a business is issuing an invoice which has a number of separate items, it should work out the VAT separately for each line of goods or services and either round each line down to the nearest 0.1 pence or round each line up or down to the nearest 1 pence or 0.5 pence.

Therefore the rule you should remember when calculating VAT is to **round down all VAT amounts, calculated to the nearest penny.** All you have to do in practice to achieve this is to remove all the numbers to the right of the pence. Set out below are some examples of VAT amounts rounded down; the numbers to be removed are shown in grey:

345.67896	becomes	345.67
29.9976	"	29.99
45.555	"	45.55

calculating VAT when it is included in the total

Sometimes you may have to deal with a low value invoice or receipt which quotes a figure which includes VAT at a certain rate, but does not actually tell you what the VAT amount is.

Let us take an example of a receipt or invoice for £12.00 for some stationery. This includes the cost of the stationery (100%) and also the VAT (assumed to be 20% for this example). The total amount therefore equates to 120% of the cost price before VAT is added on.

The formula to use in this case is:

$$\frac{the\ total\ amount\ which\ includes\ VAT}{(100\%\ +\ VAT\%)}\ \ x\ VAT\ \%$$

Applying this formula to the total figure of £12.00, the calculation is:

$$\frac{£12}{120\%}\ x\ 20\%\ =\ \text{a VAT content of £2.00}$$

Therefore the £12.00 total amount is made up of a cost price of £10.00 and VAT of £2.00 (£10.00 is £12.00 minus £2.00).

alternative method – the VAT fraction

If the VAT rate is 20%, another way of working out the VAT included in a total amount is to multiply the whole amount by what is known as the 'VAT fraction' of $1/6$. In practice, for a 20% VAT rate, all you therefore have to do is to divide the whole amount which includes VAT by 6.

The calculation for the amount of £12 is:

£12.00 ÷ 6 = £2.00.

Note that this fraction of $1/6$ only works for a VAT rate of 20%. If the VAT percentage rate is different, the fraction will be different. The fractions are published in the HMRC VAT Guide. If the rate when you are using this book is different from the 20% rate, log onto HMRC online (www.hmrc.gov.uk) and key in 'VAT fraction' in the search box to reference the section which will show the appropriate fraction.

An example of another VAT fraction is the fraction for 5% reduced rate VAT, which is $1/21$. The VAT in this case can be found by dividing the total amount (which includes VAT) by 21.

trade and settlement discounts and VAT

HMRC requires that VAT is calculated on the invoiced amount after any **trade discount** has been deducted – which is fairly obvious!

The treatment of VAT after deduction of **settlement discount** is more complicated. **Settlement discount** (also known as prompt payment discount) is a discount offered by the seller to encourage the buyer to settle up straightaway or in a short space of time rather than waiting until the due date specified on the invoice. In this case the invoice terms would include a phrase like:*"Settlement discount of 2.5% for payment within seven days"*. This means that the seller will allow 2.5% off the net invoice price (ie the price before VAT) if it is settled within seven days of the invoice date.

There are two important points to remember:

1   VAT charged on an invoice with settlement discount offered is calculated on the invoice amount **after** the discount, ie HMRC assumes that the discount will always be taken and the selling price reduced accordingly.

2   The invoice total is the sum of this reduced amount of VAT and the goods total **before** deduction of settlement discount.

If you study the invoice on the next page, you will see that the calculations for a settlement discount of 2.5% and the appropriate VAT are as follows:

Step 1	Calculate the trade discount (as normal) £236.00 x 10% (ie 10/100) = £23.60
Step 2	Calculate the net price/Goods Total (as normal) £236.00 – £23.60 = £212.40
Step 3	NOW calculate the settlement discount £212.40 x 2.5% (ie 2.5/100) = £5.31
Step 4	Calculate the reduced goods total (not written on the invoice) £212.40 – £5.31 = £207.09
Step 5	Calculate the VAT on this lower amount £207.09 x 20% (ie 20/100) = £41.41
Step 6	Calculate the total invoice price **(using the goods total before deduction of settlement discount)** £212.40 + £41.41 = £253.81

an exception to the treatment of settlement discounts and VAT

In the Finance Act 2014 the rules on settlement discounts were changed for certain businesses. If a VAT registered business supplies broadcasting or telecommunications services and offers a settlement discount, VAT must be charged on the amount actually paid by the buyer.

We will now look at an example of how this works in practice.

A customer receives an invoice from his telephone supplier for £143.10 plus VAT. The invoice states that if the customer pays within 10 days of the date of the invoice he will receive a 10% prompt payment discount. We will calculate the amount of VAT chargeable depending on whether he pays within the 10 days or not.

situation 1 – customer pays within the 10 days settlement discount period

the discounted amount = £143.10 – 10% = £143.10 – £14.31 = £128.79

the VAT payable = £128.79 x 20% = £25.75

situation 2 – customer pays outside the 10 days settlement discount period

the VAT payable = £143.10 x 20% = £28.62

INVOICE   ARTIX SUPPLIES

Unit 15 Maddox Estate, Broadfield, BR7 4ER
Tel 01908 765314 Fax 01908 765951 Email sales@artix.co.uk
VAT Reg GB 0745 4672 76

invoice to

H G Wells Limited	invoice no	787923
45 Rainbow Arcade	account	3993
Hunstanton, NR1 3RF		

deliver to

| as above | your reference | 47609 |
| | date/tax point | 02 10 20-3 |

product code	description	quantity	price £	unit	total £	discount %	net £
45B	Goya paint brushes	100	2.36	each	236.00	10.00	212.40

terms
2.5% settlement discount for payment within 7 days, otherwise 30 days after invoice date.

goods total	212.40
VAT @ 20%	41.41
TOTAL	253.81

an invoice with 10% trade discount deducted and 2.5% settlement discount allowed for quick settlement

(note that the VAT has been rounded down in the calculation)

TAX POINTS

The **tax point** of a taxable supply is the date that it is recorded as taking place for the purposes of the VAT Return.

There are different types of tax points and a business will need to ensure that it gets the right transaction on the correct VAT Return. As we will see in Chapter 4, VAT Returns are normally submitted to HMRC every three months. Complication may arise when businesses offer customers the option to pay for goods and services in different ways: for example payment in advance of delivery.

In this section we will explain how this all works in practice. The first point to note is that HM Revenue & Customs makes a distinction between **basic tax points** and **actual tax points**.

basic tax points

If a business supplies **goods**, the **basic tax point** is usually the date when:

- the supplier sends them to the customer, or
- the customer collects them, or
- the supplier makes them available for the customer to use

If you supply **services** the **basic tax point** is:

- the date when the service is performed
- normally taken as the date when all the work is completed

Whether a business supplies goods or services, the rules for basic tax points can be set aside if an **actual tax point** is created, for example an advance payment or the issue of a VAT invoice after the basic tax point.

actual tax point – advance payments

An advance payment may be made by a customer before a business supplies the goods or services. If a VAT invoice is issued or payment is received **before the basic tax point** (the supply of the goods or service) then the date of the VAT invoice or the payment – whichever happens first – becomes the **actual tax point.** For more on advance payments, see page 47.

actual tax point – 14 day rule

If a VAT invoice is issued **up to 14 days** after the basic tax point (date of supply) the date of issue of the invoice becomes the actual tax point.

This 14 day rule may be varied – with the written approval of the local VAT Office. For example, a supplier may issue monthly invoices on a regular basis for goods or services supplied during the whole of the month. The date of the invoice or the last day of the month – consistently applied – will then become the **actual tax point**.

The principle of the tax point is important to the VAT-registered business:

■ it results in a consistent and accurate method of recording VAT transactions

■ it can help cash flow in a business – an early tax point helps a business purchasing goods because the input tax can be reclaimed earlier, eg for a purchase in the last week of a VAT quarter (a VAT accounting period of 3 months), rather than in the next week – this will make a three month (VAT quarter) difference in cash flow

Chapter Summary

■ A VAT-registered supplier selling goods or services will provide a VAT invoice to the buyer; this invoice must contain certain details laid down by HM Revenue & Customs and will document the output tax charged by the seller and the input tax which the buyer may be able to claim back.

■ Supplies charged at different VAT rates on an invoice must show as separate items with all VAT rates and amounts shown separately.

■ There are certain variations on the type of invoice that may be used: if the amount of the invoice is less than £250, a less detailed invoice may be used which does not show the VAT amount separately.

■ Businesses that supply goods and services to other states in the European Union will issue an EU customer invoice which will contain the buyer's VAT registration number.

■ A pro-forma invoice (used to request payment in advance) is not, however, classed as a VAT invoice.

■ Businesses dealing with VAT may need to carry out a variety of calculations when dealing with VAT documentation, including working out the VAT content of an amount which includes VAT, and VAT on settlement (prompt payment) discount. Manual calculations of VAT totals can be rounded down to the nearest penny.

■ When VAT-registered businesses complete a VAT Return they must ensure that the time of the supply of goods and services for tax purposes – the tax point – is accurately recorded as it can affect the timing of payment of output tax and claims for input tax.

VAT invoice	an invoice issued by a VAT-registered supplier which must contain certain details, including: – a consecutive invoice number and the date (which is normally the tax point) – the seller's name and address – the seller's VAT registration number – the buyer's name and address – a description of the goods or services – unit price and quantity – cost before VAT, VAT amount, total amount – VAT rate and total of VAT
simplified invoice	an invoice for £250 or less which does not have to show the VAT amount(s) charged separately
pro-forma invoice	a document issued by a supplier, inviting a buyer to pay for goods before they are supplied – this document is not a VAT invoice
VAT receipt	a document issued for a cash sale, often by a retailer, which shows the name, address and VAT registration number of the supplier and the VAT amounts and rates of the goods or services sold
EU customer invoice	a VAT invoice issued to a customer in another EU state; it must show the VAT registration number of the customer
rounding rules	VAT can be rounded down to the nearest penny
VAT fraction	the fraction used to work out the VAT content of an amount which contains VAT
settlement discount VAT	the VAT on early settlement discount is calculated on the assumption that the discount will be taken – whether or not it actually is taken; the exception is for broadcasting and telecommunications providers who must calculate VAT on the amount paid by the customer
tax point	the date on which the supply is recorded for the purposes of the VAT Return – normally the date of the invoice
basic tax point	the date on which the goods are sent or collected or the service performed (also normally the invoice date)
actual tax point	any variation to the basic tax point, for example if advance payment is made or the 14 day rule applied
14 day rule	if a VAT invoice is issued up to 14 days after the basic tax point, the date of issue becomes the tax point

Activities

2.1   A VAT invoice for goods sent by a seller to a buyer within the UK must contain the following items:

(a)   invoice number, purchase order number, seller's name, seller's VAT registration number

(b)   invoice number, invoice date, buyer's name, buyer's VAT registration number

(c)   invoice number, amount of VAT charged, unit price, VAT rate

(d)   invoice number, seller's address, unit price, buyer's VAT registration number

Which **ONE** of these options is correct?

2.2   A VAT invoice for goods sent by a seller in the UK to a buyer in an EU state must contain the following items:

(a)   invoice number, purchase order number, seller's name, seller's VAT registration number

(b)   invoice number, seller's name, buyer's name, buyer's VAT registration number

(c)   invoice number, amount of VAT charged, unit price, currency conversion rate

(d)   invoice number, seller's name, seller's email address, VAT rate

Which **ONE** of these options is correct?

2.3   If a VAT invoice for goods sent by a seller in the UK covers the sale of two items, one zero-rated and the other standard-rated, the invoice should:

(a)   show the two items on separate lines of the invoice with separate VAT rates and separate VAT amounts

(b)   only show the VAT amount for the standard-rated item because there is no VAT charged on the zero-rated item

(c)   only show the the standard-rated item because there is no need for a VAT invoice for a zero-rated supply

(d)   charge VAT at an average rate worked out by adding the two rates together and dividing the total by two

Which **ONE** of these options is correct?

2.4   A 'simplified invoice' can be used when:

(a)   the supplier is not registered for VAT

(b)   the buyer is not registered for VAT

(c)   the supplies are zero-rated and so no VAT is involved

(d)   the amount involved is £250 or less

Which **ONE** of these options is correct?

2.5 You work in the accounts department of a local carpet store and a salesperson who is new to the job hands you a slip of paper, saying:

'Here's a VAT receipt for some petrol I bought on company business – I have been told to hand it in so that you can get the VAT back.'

Would you accept it? If not, why not? State two things that are wrong with it.

```
┌─────────────────────────────────────────┐
│                                          │
│       ASCO SUPERMARKETS PLC              │
│            Liverpool LP5 4FT             │
│                                          │
│                                          │
│   Your operator today is JAMIE           │
│   13/05/20-6 at 12.03 pm                 │
│   Shift 986                              │
│   Transaction number 9479474 Till No 5   │
│                                          │
│   Bread rolls (six pack)      £1.25      │
│                                          │
│   Pump 9: Unleaded                       │
│   35.90 L @ 129.9             £46.63     │
│                                          │
│   TOTAL                       £47.88     │
│                                          │
│   PAID by VISA                £47.88     │
│   ICC 412848******3756                   │
│                                          │
│                                          │
│   POINTS CARD                            │
│   Points accumulated      2056           │
│   Points this transaction  430           │
│   Total Points            2486           │
│                                          │
│   THANK YOU FOR SHOPPING AT ASCO         │
│                                          │
└─────────────────────────────────────────┘
```

2.6 A pro-forma invoice is issued by a business selling goods so that:

(a) the buyer can use it to claim back the input VAT on the goods

(b) the buyer can deduct settlement discount if payment is made within seven days

(c) the buyer can send a payment in advance to obtain the goods

(d) the buyer can avoid paying the VAT normally due on the goods

Which **ONE** of these options is correct?

2.7 You are working out the VAT total on a UK invoice and the calculator shows an amount of £34.78954. This should be rounded to a figure of:

(a) £34.789

(b) £34.78

(c) £34.79

(d) £35.00

Which **ONE** of these options is correct?

2.8   You work in the accounts department of a local business and are handed a receipt for payment for some stationery costing £23.44. There is no VAT amount shown on the receipt because the shop which sold the goods claimed that their till did not 'show VAT' as it was already included in all their prices. The current rate of VAT is 20%. You work out the VAT content to be:

(a)   £3.90

(b)   £3.91

(c)   £4.68

(d)   £19.53

Which **ONE** of these options is correct?

2.9   You are preparing a VAT invoice for a customer and have been asked by your line manager to add the option for the customer to take settlement discount at 2.5% for settlement within 7 days. The goods total after trade discount and before the deduction of settlement discount is £118.00.

Assuming a 20% VAT rate, the VAT charged and the final total of the invoice will be:

(a)   VAT of £23.60, invoice total £138.65

(b)   VAT of £23.60, invoice total £141.60

(c)   VAT of £23.01, invoice total £141.01

(d)   VAT of £23.01, invoice total £138.06

Which **ONE** of these options is correct?

2.10   A customer receives a telephone bill dated 27 July for £98 plus VAT. The terms of the bill are that a 10% discount will be applied if the customer settles within 10 days. The customer pays the bill on 12 August.

Assuming a 20% VAT rate, the VAT charge and the final total of the invoice will be:

(a)   VAT of £19.60, invoice total £107.80

(b)   VAT of £19.60, invoice total £117.60

(c)   VAT of £17.64, invoice total £115.64

(d)   VAT of £17.64, invoice total £105.84

Which **ONE** of the options is correct?

2.11   The basic VAT tax point for a supplier selling goods is when:

(a)   the customer orders the goods

(b)   the goods are sent to the customer

(c)   the date the customer pays for the goods

(d)   the date the next VAT Return is completed by the supplier

Which **ONE** of these options is correct?

2.12   The actual VAT tax point for a supplier selling goods, receiving payment in full 21 days in advance of supply and issuing a VAT invoice 7 days in advance of the supply, is:

(a)   the date of the payment

(b)   the date of the VAT invoice

(c)   the date the customer receives the goods

(d)   the date the next VAT Return is completed by the supplier

Which **ONE** of these options is correct?

3 Inputs and outputs and special schemes

this chapter covers...

This chapter describes further aspects of inputs and outputs and input tax and output tax. It explains why it is important to get the timing of these inputs and outputs correct for the completion of the VAT Return. The specific areas covered include:

■ the difference between input VAT and output VAT

■ the different rates of VAT

■ the difference between zero-rated supplies and exempt supplies when it comes to reclaiming input tax

■ the subject of partial exemption, which is where a business supplies both taxable goods or services and also exempt goods or services and so cannot normally reclaim all the input tax paid

■ the way in which businesses should account for VAT on business entertainment

■ the VAT situation which relates to the sale and purchase of cars and vans, reclaiming VAT paid on fuel used by cars and the need to pay fuel scale charges

■ how the payment of VAT is affected by customers putting down deposits and making advance payments for supplies of goods and services

This chapter then explains how imports and exports of goods and services are treated for VAT purposes. It also describes how the VAT situation is different depending on whether the countries are part of the European Union (EU) or are outside Europe.

Lastly, this chapter describes the various special schemes for payment of VAT, including the annual accounting scheme, the flat rate scheme and the cash accounting scheme.

OUTPUT VAT AND INPUT VAT – SOME REVISION

output VAT and input VAT – definitions

Input tax is the VAT a business is charged on its business purchases and expenses.

Output tax is the VAT that is due to HM Revenue & Customs on supplies of goods or services made by a business.

output VAT and input VAT – the rates

The rates of VAT charged at the time of writing this text are:

- **standard rate**   20%

- **reduced rate**   5%

- **zero rate**   0%

These rates of VAT (apart from zero rate) can change from time-to-time.

output VAT and input VAT – the calculation

The VAT amount due to HM Revenue & Customs from a VAT-registered business is calculated in the VAT Return as: **output tax less input tax**.

HM Revenue & Customs will therefore want to ensure that a VAT-registered business:

- **charges** the correct amount of output tax – this is comparatively straightforward as it is calculated by applying the appropriate percentage rate to the taxable supply of goods or services

- **claims** the correct amount of input tax (and no more than the correct amount) to offset against the output VAT it charges – here the regulations are more complex, as we will explain in this chapter

A further aspect to consider in relation to input tax is the **timing of a claim**. It is obviously in the interest of the buyer of goods or services to claim as soon as possible for any input VAT incurred as this will help the cash flow of the business.

This timing is normally based, as we saw in the last chapter, on the **tax point** of the transaction. This is normally the date of the invoice issued for the supply of the goods or services.

There are, however, variations on this timing, either through a variation in the tax point and also through VAT Special Schemes, which are explained at the end of this Chapter.

ZERO-RATED AND EXEMPT SUPPLIES

the difference

Zero-rated goods and services, eg books and food, are chargeable to output VAT, but at zero per cent, so effectively no VAT is charged. A supplier of zero-rated goods and services, that is registered for VAT, will be able to reclaim input VAT spent on business purchases and expenses. Therefore, when a supplier of zero-rated goods and services completes a VAT Return, the calculation of output VAT (zero) minus input VAT (a positive amount) results in a negative figure. This means that HM Revenue & Customs will then owe the business this amount and will make a VAT refund. This will normally be sent electronically direct to the bank account of the business, giving a useful boost to the cash flow of the supplier.

For **suppliers of goods and services that are VAT-exempt**, for example providers of educational courses and healthcare, the situation is very different. Suppliers of VAT-exempt goods and services are not able to reclaim input VAT.

In conclusion, the rule to remember is:

■ suppliers of **zero-rated** goods and services should register for VAT and will be able to reclaim input VAT that they pay on business supplies

■ suppliers of **VAT-exempt** goods and services cannot reclaim the input VAT that they pay on business supplies

TAXABLE AND EXEMPT SUPPLIES – PARTIAL EXEMPTION

the problem

The VAT regulations state that normally if a business is registered for VAT and makes

■ **some** supplies that are VAT-exempt and

■ **some** supplies that are taxable (eg standard-rated)

then that business will not be able to reclaim the input VAT it has paid on the purchases that relate to the exempt supplies it has made.

HM Revenue & Customs, however, states that if the amount of VAT incurred relating to exempt supplies is below a certain amount (known as the '**de minimis**' limit) input VAT can be recovered in full.

We will now explain both these situations.

partial exemption – how to work out the input tax

If a business makes both taxable and exempt supplies and has to pay input tax that relates to both kinds of supply, the business will be classified as '**partly exempt**'. Unless the business qualifies under the 'de minimis' rules (see next page) it will have to make a calculation which works out how much input tax it can recover to set off against its output VAT when it completes its VAT Return.

We will take as an imaginary example – Speakeasy Limited – a business that runs educational courses and sells DVDs.

Speakeasy has annual taxable sales of over the annual threshold and so the business is VAT-registered. It has two main products:

- intensive English language courses for overseas students coming to the UK – these courses are VAT-exempt under HMRC regulations because they are providing an educational service

- the 'Speakeasy' series of foreign language DVDs which are standard-rated for VAT under HMRC regulations because they are taxable supplies

How does Speakeasy sort out its VAT Return?

output VAT is relatively straightforward:

- it is only charged on the DVDs, which are standard-rated

- it is not charged on the language courses because they are VAT-exempt

input VAT is rather more complicated:

- when it is charged on purchases and expenses directly related to providing language courses, it **cannot be reclaimed as input tax** because it relates to the provision of exempt supplies, ie the language courses

- when it is charged on purchases and expenses directly related to producing the DVDs, it **can be claimed as input tax** because it relates to standard-rated supplies, ie the DVDs that Speakeasy sells

But the problem is that there are also some purchases and expenses which **cannot be directly related to either courses or to DVDs**, for example telephone bills and administration costs.

The input tax charged on these supplies is known as 'residual input tax' and **some of it** may be recovered according to the proportion of the company's sales of taxable supplies (the DVDs) to the total of all its supplies.

So, if £36,000 of Speakeasy's total supplies of £120,000 were taxable (ie the sale of its DVDs), the percentage of the residual input VAT which could be claimed back and set against output VAT would be:

$$\frac{£36,000 \times 100}{£120,000} = 30\%$$

You will not have to carry out these calculations in your assessments, but you will need to appreciate the underlying principles.

partial exemption – the 'de minimis' limit

The use of the **'de minimis' limit** allows a business to recover **all** the input VAT charged on taxable **and exempt** purchases and expenses if the total value of that input tax is less than a set amount – ie the 'de minimis' limit.

In other words, HM Revenue & Customs allows businesses which sell a mix of taxable supplies (eg standard-rated goods) and VAT-exempt supplies to avoid the hard work involved in all the calculations for partial exemption described on the previous page. They are allowed to take into account in the VAT Returns **all the input tax** related to their exempt supplies.

But this is only permissable **if the amount of input tax to be deducted is insignificant**. The meaning of the phrase 'de minimis' is 'this is so small that it is really not worth bothering about'. There are a number of HMRC tests to work out if the amount of input tax relating to exempt supplies is small enough to qualify for 'de minimis', One of these, introduced in 2010, states that a business can deduct all the input tax related to its exempt supplies if the total input tax incurred is less than £625 per month on average and total exempt supplies do not exceed 50% of total supplies.

BUSINESS EXPENSES

It is important to appreciate that businesses can only claim back VAT which has been charged on costs and expenses incurred which are **business expenses**.

If a business uses goods or services partly for business purposes and partly for non-business purposes the business must work out a realistic split between business and non-business when calculating a claim for input VAT.

business entertainment

HM Revenue & Customs states that a business **cannot recover input tax related to business entertainment expenses**. Although a business can normally recover, as input tax, VAT incurred on goods or services used for a business purpose, claims for refund of input tax charged on business entertainment is prohibited (except for overseas visitors) under a special legal provision.

Entertainment is 'business entertainment' when it is provided to people who are not employees of the business and it is provided free. The following are examples of business entertainment:

- provision of food and drink, eg meals in restaurants
- provision of accommodation, eg in hotels
- theatre and concert tickets
- entry to sporting events and facilities

■ entry to clubs and nightclubs

■ use of facilities such as yachts and aircraft for the purpose of entertaining

Note that business entertainment should not be confused with **employee entertainment**. If a business provides entertainment to reward employees for good work or to improve staff morale, it is considered to be for business purposes and the input VAT can be reclaimed. Examples of employee entertainment include seasonal staff parties and staff outings.

mixed entertaining

When a business entertains employees and clients together, it may be able to claim back some of the VAT. In this case clients may be customers, potential customers or suppliers of the business. The proportion of VAT that does not relate to client entertaining and that is used for business purposes can be reclaimed. For example if a business entertains employees, customers and/or suppliers together, it may be able to reclaim the proportion of the expenses that relate to employee entertainment. However, none of the VAT can be reclaimed if the sole purpose of the business entertainment is to entertain the non-employee. For example if several members of staff take a client out for a round of golf none of the VAT can be claimed.

VEHICLES AND VAT

car and van purchase

Businesses are not normally able to reclaim the input VAT when they buy a **car**. But they are able to reclaim all of the VAT if:

■ the car will be used exclusively for business purposes and is not available for private use by employees or family – not even for driving to work

■ the business is a taxi business, a driving school or provides self-drive hire cars

■ the business is a car dealer and the car will be part of its inventory (stock) that it intends to sell within the next 12 months

The good news is that a business can reclaim all the VAT charged on vehicle repairs and maintenance as long as:

■ the business pays for the work

■ there is some business use of the vehicle

Businesses can, however, reclaim in the normal way the input VAT paid on the purchase of **commercial vehicles** such as **vans**.

car and van sale

If a business was not able to reclaim the input VAT on the original purchase price of a car which was bought new, it will not have to charge any VAT when the car is sold.

If a business such as a driving school wishes to sell a car for which it was able to reclaim the input VAT when it bought it, it will have to charge VAT on the full selling price of the car and issue a VAT invoice to a VAT-registered buyer if they ask for one.

If a business buys or sells second-hand vehicles it may choose to use a **VAT margin scheme**. This enables it to account for VAT on the difference between the price paid for the vehicle and the price at which it is sold, in other words it is VAT charged on the profit or 'margin'.

Note, however, that some commercial vehicles, such as **vans**, cannot be sold under the margin scheme. The definition of cars eligible for the scheme is contained in the Value Added Tax (Cars) Order 1992.

reclaiming VAT on road fuel

Businesses commonly buy or lease cars for use by their employees; these are often known as 'company cars' and are usually made available to employees for private motoring as well as business use.

If a business pays for road fuel used by employees, there are a number of different ways in which it can deal with the VAT charged on the fuel:

- the business need not reclaim any input VAT at all – this can be a useful option if the annual mileage of the vehicle is very low and if the fuel is used for both business and private motoring
- if the fuel is used only for business purposes (which does not include driving to work), the business can reclaim all of the input VAT charged
- if the fuel is used for business purposes and for private motoring the business can reclaim only the VAT that relates to fuel used for business mileage – this means that the business (and the employee) needs to keep detailed records of business and private mileage
- if the fuel is used for business purposes and for private motoring the business can reclaim all of the VAT charged and then pay a separate **fuel scale charge** (see below)

fuel scale charge

Businesses purchasing fuel which will be used for both business and private motoring can account for VAT by:

- reclaiming all the VAT charged, and
- paying a **fuel scale charge** to HM Revenue & Customs

The fuel scale charge is a quarterly charge on the CO_2 (carbon dioxide) emissions of vehicles: the higher the emissions, the greater the pollution level, and the higher the fuel scale charge. This charge has a political agenda: the Government can be seen to be environmentally friendly because it is effectively taxing atmospheric pollution.

Fuel scale charge rates tend to go up every year. 'Gas guzzling' cars can generally be charged a rate which is over three times as much as the charge for a low emission vehicle.

DEPOSITS, ADVANCE PAYMENTS AND PAYING BY INSTALMENTS

In some circumstances a business might offer its customers the option to pay for goods and services by:

- advance payment in full
- putting down a deposit to reserve an item
- paying in instalments

A business needs to account for VAT correctly for all these situations and will need to know how to fix the correct tax point for the VAT Return.

advance payment and deposits

An advance payment, or deposit, is a proportion of the total selling price that a customer pays before a business supplies the goods or services. If a business asks for an advance payment or deposit, the tax point is the earlier of:

- the date of the issue of a VAT invoice for the advance payment or deposit
- the date the business receives the advance payment or deposit

A business will include the VAT on the advance payment or deposit on the VAT Return for the period when the tax point for the advance payment or deposit occurs.

If the customer then pays the remaining balance before the goods are delivered or the services are provided, another tax point is created which is the earlier of the following:

- the date of the issue of a VAT invoice for the balance
- the date the business receives payment of the balance

The VAT on the balance is accounted for on the VAT Return for the period when the tax point for the balance occurs.

receiving payment by instalment

A business may allow a customer to pay for goods by instalments over an agreed period of time. The goods remain the property of the business until the full price is paid. This is known as a '**conditional sale**' – in other words, the business is saying 'the goods will be yours when you have finished paying for them; until then they remain our property'.

The basic tax point for a conditional sale is created when the goods are handed over to the customer. On that date a business should account for the VAT on the **full value** of the goods.

IMPORTS AND EXPORTS

So far we have dealt with VAT as it affects business dealings within the UK. VAT must also be accounted for in dealings with overseas states, both within the EU (European Union, formerly European Community) and also outside the EU.

The basic principle, which applies to exports and imports, is that VAT is a tax on imported goods and some services – it is paid where appropriate by the importer and is treated as an input tax.

VAT and countries outside the EU

- when goods are **imported** into the UK from countries outside the EU, VAT is normally due at the same rate that would apply to a supply of those goods within the UK – it is treated in the same way as input tax and will normally have to be paid before the goods are released by HM Revenue & Customs

- when goods are **exported** from the UK to countries outside the EU, the goods are normally zero-rated, as long as documentary evidence of export is obtained and retained by the supplier

VAT and the Single Market (the EU)

The 'Single Market' is the phrase used to describe trading within the states that make up the European Union (EU). Since the beginning of 1993 the EU has become an area in which movements of goods are no longer called 'imports' and 'exports' but 'acquisitions' or 'dispatches'. VAT is no longer collected at the frontiers but from the **buyer**:

- **if the buyer is VAT-registered** – the goods are zero-rated on despatch and VAT is collected from the buyer at the rate which applies in the buyer's country and accounted for on the buyer's VAT Return as input tax

- **if the buyer is not VAT-registered** – the goods will normally be charged by the supplier at the VAT rate which applies in the country of the supplier

the conditions for zero-rating of EU supplies

In the first case above – the supply of goods from one EU state to another between two VAT-registered businesses or individuals – the goods can only be zero-rated by a UK supplier if certain conditions are met:

- the buyer's valid VAT registration number must be obtained by the supplier and quoted on the VAT invoice – the number must include the two letter country prefix (eg DE for Germany, GB for Great Britain)
- the goods are sent to a destination in another EU state
- the supplier holds documentary evidence that the goods have been sent

A customer EU invoice is illustrated on page 29. Note the inclusion of the EU buyer's VAT registration number with the country two letter prefix.

tax points for goods supplied to the EU

The tax point for goods despatched by a UK supplier to another EU state is the earlier of:

- the date on the invoice covering the goods
- the 15th of the month following the month of supply

tax treatment for goods sent to UK buyers

When a UK buyer receives goods from another EU state:

- the tax point follows the same rules as above (ie the date of the invoice received or the 15th of the month following supply)
- VAT is payable at the rate applicable to those goods within the UK (eg books will be zero-rated, adult clothes will be standard-rated) – the amount will be entered on the VAT Return

free zones and warehousing

Mention must be made of warehousing and free zones. These are storage facilities for goods, normally at or near ports and airports; they can be used for storage of goods received from overseas.

No VAT is due on these goods until the goods are released from storage to the UK buyer. Goods received from EU states, as mentioned above, are not **imports** but **acquisitions** and are not subject to the import requirements imposed on non-EU goods.

Single Market documentation – sales lists

UK VAT-registered traders who supply other EU states with goods are required to send lists of their EU supplies to HM Revenue & Customs, normally on a quarterly basis. The standard form VAT 101 is shown on the next page.

Traders with low volumes of EU sales may be exempted from completing these forms and can obtain permission to submit a simplified annual EU Sales List.

HM Revenue & Customs

Value Added Tax EC Sales List

Please enter your name and address

Please enter the following details. If you don't, we won't be able to use the information you give on the rest of this form.

VAT Registration Number

Branch/subsidiary identifier   Period reference

To avoid a penalty, please make sure this form reaches HMRC **within 14 days** of the period end date.

Period for goods from _____ to _____

Period for services from _____ to _____

If you move, transfer supply or sell services to other EU countries you have to complete an EC Sales List. If you have not been involved in any such transactions during this period, you do not need to complete this form.

If you file your EC Sales List online, you will get an extra seven days to do so. To find out more go to www.hmrc.gov.uk and under *do it online*, select *VAT Online*.

Before you start, please enter your details at the top of this page. Please leave blank any boxes that don't apply to you.

For further advice go to www.hmrc.gov.uk or phone our Helpline on **0845 010 9000** (Monday to Friday 8am to 8pm).

Country	Customer VAT Registration Number	Total value of supplies in pounds sterling	Indicator

More...

Declaration You, or someone on your behalf, must sign below.

I declare that the information given on this form and any continuation sheets is correct and complete to the best of my knowledge.

Signature

Contact number   *In case we need to speak to you*

Full name of signatory in capital letters

Date   *DD MM YYYY*

Number of pages to this list

1

VAT101(i)   PAGE 1   HMRC 10/09

EC Sales List VAT Form 101

SPECIAL SCHEMES

HM Revenue & Customs has introduced a number of special schemes which vary the way in which VAT is collected. They are designed to help businesses which may be put at a disadvantage if VAT is collected in the normal way. They include the annual accounting scheme, the flat rate scheme and the cash accounting scheme. These are described in the next few pages.

ANNUAL ACCOUNTING SCHEME

This scheme enables businesses to make VAT Returns **annually** rather than quarterly. This is a great advantage to the small trader for whom time is valuable.

The main features of the scheme are:

- it is available to traders with an annual taxable turnover of up to £1.35 million at the time the scheme starts
- taxable turnover includes supplies at standard, reduced or zero-rated VAT, but excludes the VAT itself
- the scheme can be operated in conjunction with the flat rate scheme (see next page), or the cash accounting scheme, but not both
- if annual taxable turnover goes over £1.35 million, the trader can continue on this scheme until taxable turnover reaches £1.6 million
- the trader must pay 90% of an estimate made of the likely annual VAT payment, normally electronically by nine equal monthly instalments starting in the fourth month of the VAT year
- alternatively the trader can pay using three interim payments, each of 25% of the previous year's VAT liability or 25% of the likely annual VAT liability if the business has been VAT-registered for less than 12 months. This is payable in months 4, 7 and 10 of the annual accounting period
- the trader must pay the balance due with the annual electronic VAT Return, due two months after the end of the VAT year

The timing of the payments made is summarised in the table below.

Months	1	2	3	4	5	6	7	8	9	10	11	12	13	14
Payments (9 interim)				1	2	3	4	5	6	7	8	9		10
Payments (3 interim)				1			2			3				4

Full details of this scheme are contained in the 'Annual Accounting' guide available on www.hmrc.gov.uk as Notice 732.

advantages and disadvantages

There are a number of **advantages** of the annual accounting scheme, especially for the smaller business:

- the scheme helps a business smooth out its cash flow by paying a set amount each month, or quarter
- a business only needs to submit one VAT Return each year, instead of four
- a business is allowed two months instead of one to complete and submit the online annual VAT Return and send the balancing payment

The main disadvantage is if you regularly reclaim VAT (if you supply zero-rated goods such as books) you only get one repayment of VAT each year.

FLAT RATE SCHEME

The **flat rate scheme** is designed for small businesses whose annual taxable turnover does not exceed £150,000, and whose total turnover (including income on which no VAT is paid) does not exceed £230,000 a year.

It is radically different from normal VAT schemes in which input VAT and output VAT are identified and recorded, resulting either in net VAT being paid over to HM Revenue & Customs, or reclaimed (if tax on expenses [inputs] is greater than that on sales [outputs]).

With the **flat rate scheme** the business does not have to identify and record every single VAT transaction in order to calculate the net amount of VAT due. Instead a **flat percentage rate** is charged on the total supplies (sales) for each VAT period. This calculation produces the amount of VAT due.

The flat rate varies with the trade sectors. Some common examples are shown in the table below.

type of business	flat rate
retailers of food and newspapers	4%
sports facilities	8.5%
photography	11%
entertainment	12.5%
pubs	6.5%
bookkeeping services	14.5%

A benefit of the flat rate scheme is that a business in its first year of VAT registration gets a 1% reduction in its applicable flat rate percentage for 12 months after registration.

The calculation of the flat rate VAT is simple. Suppose you are a bookkeeper and your quarterly supplies (ie income from customers) is £24,000, including VAT. Your flat rate is 14.5% and so your quarterly VAT liability is:

$$£24,000 \ \text{x} \ 14.5\% \ = \ £3,480$$

If you ran a photography studio and your quarterly turnover was also £24,000, your VAT liability (see table on previous page) would be:

$$£24,000 \ \text{x} \ 11\% \ = \ £2,640$$

Remember that the flat rate is used only to calculate the amount of VAT you owe, because an allowance is made for input tax in the percentage. **You will not charge VAT at the flat rate**, but instead at the normal rate for the supplies. You will issue VAT invoices showing the normal VAT rate charged.

Also, if your supplies are **zero-rated** (for example if you sell books) and you normally reclaim VAT because your inputs are higher than your outputs, you would not use the flat rate scheme (unless you want to give money away!)

Another point to note is that if you purchase a **capital asset**, eg a computer, with an invoice value (including VAT) of £2,000 or more, you can claim the input VAT paid on this asset. If you sell it again, you will have to charge VAT at full rate and pay back to HM Revenue & Customs the VAT you receive. This extra VAT on purchases (inputs) and sales (outputs) will be recorded on the VAT Return, which is due quarterly (unless the flat rate scheme is operated in conjunction with the annual accounting scheme – see below).

The records that you will need to keep for the flat rate scheme are:

- the flat rate turnover for the VAT accounting period
- the flat rate percentage used
- the VAT calculated as due
- a VAT account – recording VAT paid under the scheme and any VAT involved in the purchase or sale of a capital asset

Note that the flat rate scheme may be operated with the annual accounting scheme. This makes dealing with VAT far simpler for the small business. Not only is VAT calculated as a basic percentage, it is only calculated once a year. Details of the scheme are available on www.hmrc.gov.uk as Notice 733.

CASH ACCOUNTING SCHEME

This scheme allows businesses to account for VAT on the basis of the date of **payments** received and made rather than on the tax point on **invoices** received and issued.

In other words a business under this scheme does not have to account for output tax on the date of the supply, but only when (and if!) payment is received, which could be many months later. This is an enormous help to traders who have to pay their suppliers promptly but may have to wait a long time before receiving payment.

It also provides automatic relief for VAT on bad debts: if the buyer does not pay up, no output VAT is declarable (as it would be if VAT was assessable on invoices rather than payments). To qualify for this scheme a business must:

- anticipate annual taxable turnover of £1.35 million or less – this includes taxable supplies at standard rate, reduced rate and zero rate, but excludes VAT itself and exempt supplies
- have a 'clean' VAT record – ie all VAT Returns made on time, no assessments for VAT evasion or convictions for VAT fraud

If a supplier starts to use the cash accounting scheme and annual taxable turnover exceeds £1.35 million, the supplier can carry on using the scheme until annual taxable turnover reaches £1.6 million.

When registered under this scheme a supplier will continue to issue VAT invoices but will need to keep accounting records in a specific way:

- the tax point for payments in cash, by cheque, credit card, bank transfer is always the transaction date (eg the date on the credit card voucher)
- a cash book (or similar record) must be maintained summarising all payments made and received, with a separate column for VAT, suitable for providing the data for the VAT Return
- invoices issued or received for any payments made in cash must be receipted and dated

The cash accounting scheme cannot be operated in conjunction with the flat rate scheme. Details of the cash accounting scheme are available at www.hmrc.gov.uk (Notice 731).

A NOTE ON RETAIL SCHEMES

VAT accounting for shops who may make a mixture of standard-rated, zero-rated and exempt supplies is potentially very complex. HM Revenue & Customs has introduced a series of **retail schemes** to help retail suppliers work out VAT on taxable supplies at different rates at the till.

You do not at this stage in your studies need to know all the 'ins and outs' of retail schemes, but you should note that they are available and also that the flat rate scheme cannot be used in conjunction with a retail scheme, but it has its own 'retailer's method' of calculation as an option.

Chapter Summary

- Input tax is the VAT a business is charged on its business purchases and expenses – it can often be reclaimed; output tax is the VAT that is due to HM Revenue & Customs on supplies of goods or services made.

- Different types of taxable supplies of goods and services will be charged at a variety of different rates, which include: standard rate, reduced rate and zero rate. Exempt supplies are not charged at any rate at all.

- The difference between zero-rated and exempt supplies is that suppliers who are VAT-registered and sell zero-rated supplies can reclaim input VAT whereas sellers of VAT-exempt supplies cannot reclaim input VAT.

- Partial exemption is the situation where a supplier sells a mix of VAT-rated and exempt goods and services and has to calculate how much input tax it can reclaim on the basis of the amount of VAT-rated goods sold. The exception to this is where the amount of exempt input tax is insignificant and can be reclaimed anyway under the 'de minimis' rule.

- Businesses can only reclaim input tax where the expense involved is a business expense. Business entertainment – eg free entertainment to customers – is not classed as a business expense and the input tax cannot be reclaimed.

- The input VAT charged on vehicles bought by a business cannot be reclaimed unless the vehicle is being solely used for business purposes. If a business sells a car on which no VAT was reclaimed, it will not have to charge VAT on the sale.

- If a business buys fuel for its vehicles which are only used for business purposes, it may reclaim the input VAT; if the vehicle is also used for private purposes the business may only reclaim all the VAT if it pays a fuel scale charge based on the vehicle's emissions.

- If a business sells goods or services and asks for payment in advance, a deposit or payment by instalments, the tax point for calculation of VAT is generally fixed when each payment is made or invoiced.

- If VAT-registered businesses buy and sell within the EU the goods will be zero-rated on dispatch and the VAT collected from the buyer. These goods are not exports but 'acquisitions'. Goods exported to a country outside the EU should be zero-rated.

- To help businesses which may be put at a disadvantage by the standard VAT Return system, HM Revenue & Customs has introduced a number of special schemes to help businesses: annual accounting scheme, flat rate scheme, and cash accounting scheme.

partial exemption	the situation where a business makes both taxable and exempt supplies and has to calculate the amount of input tax it can reclaim, based on the extent of its taxable supplies
'de minimis' limit	where the amount of input tax which relates to a supplier's exempt supplies – which the supplier could not normally reclaim – is so insignificant that HMRC allows the business to reclaim it
business entertainment	entertainment provided free of charge to people who are not employees of a business – food, drink, accommodation, theatre, sport, clubbing
margin scheme	accounting for VAT on the difference between the price paid for an item (eg car) and the price at which it is sold, ie the profit 'margin'
fuel scale charge	a quarterly charge on the CO_2 emissions of a vehicle to offset the claiming back of input VAT paid on fuel used by a company vehicle
acquisition	the sale and purchase of goods or services within the EU
exports and imports	the sale and purchase of goods in countries outside the EU
annual accounting scheme	a scheme which enables businesses (with annual taxable turnover of £1.35 million or less) to make VAT Returns annually rather than quarterly – VAT owing is paid in regular instalments and the VAT Return is due two months after the end of the VAT period
flat rate scheme	a scheme which enables businesses with an annual taxable turnover of up to £150,000 to pay VAT at a flat percentage rate based on tax inclusive turnover
cash accounting scheme	a scheme which allows businesses (with annual taxable turnover of £1.35M or less) to account for VAT on the basis of payments received and made rather than the tax point on invoices received and issued; it provides automatic relief for VAT on bad debts

Activities

3.1   A business will be unable to reclaim input VAT if its supplies are:

(a)   zero-rated

(b)   exempt

(c)   standard-rated

(d)   reduced-rated

Which **ONE** of these options is correct?

3.2   A business that is partially exempt supplies:

(a)   some goods that are zero-rated and some that are standard-rated

(b)   some goods that are zero-rated and some that are reduced-rated

(c)   some goods that are standard-rated and some that are exempt

(d)   some goods that are standard-rated and some that are reduced-rated

Which **ONE** of these options is correct?

3.3   Residual input tax is the VAT that:

(a)   is charged on costs and expenses that cannot definitely be attributed to standard-rated supplies or to exempt supplies

(b)   is charged on costs and expenses that have not been settled at the end of the VAT accounting period

(c)   is charged on costs and expenses that can definitely be attributed to standard-rated supplies or to zero-rated supplies

(d)   is charged on costs and expenses that have been settled before the due date in order to obtain settlement discount

Which **ONE** of these options is correct?

3.4   A 'de minimis' limit:

(a)   is the amount set for the lowest rate of the fuel scale charge levied on very small cars

(b)   is the annual sales turnover limit set for registration for partial exemption

(c)   is the annual sales turnover limit set for VAT registration for a business making exempt supplies

(d)   is the limit set which enables a partially exempt business to reclaim input VAT paid on exempt supplies

Which **ONE** of these options is correct?

3.5   Your business will be able to deduct input VAT on the VAT Return in the following circumstances:

(a)   you fill up your company car with fuel when driving home (no fuel scale charge is paid)

(b)   you take a small group of customers for a night out at a local club

(c)   you take a group of customers to an international rugby match

(d)   you take out your staff for a celebration meal

Which **ONE** of these options is correct?

3.6   A business buying a car can deduct input VAT charged on the car when:

(a)   the car will be used by the managing director and his family

(b)   the car is used by a salesperson for business trips only and is kept at the employee's home

(c)   the business is a car hire firm and the car will be hired out to customers

(d)   the car is mostly used for business purposes but is occasionally used by employees at the weekend out of business hours

Which **ONE** of these options is correct?

3.7   When a VAT-registered business supplies goods to a VAT-registered buyer in another EU state, it must:

(a)   charge VAT at the standard rate because the goods are standard-rated in the other EU state

(b)   not charge VAT at all because the transaction takes place within the EU

(c)   charge VAT at a rate which is the sum of the two countries' VAT rates added together

(d)   zero rate the goods so that input VAT can be collected from the buyer in the other EU state

Which **ONE** of these options is correct?

3.8   The annual accounting scheme requires that:

(a)   the VAT Return has to be submitted every 12 months

(b)   taxable turnover must be at standard rate or at reduced rate

(c)   the VAT payment only needs to be made to HM Revenue & Customs every twelve months

(d)   the VAT payment has to be made in twelve equal monthly instalments

Which **ONE** of these options is correct?

3.9   The flat rate scheme requires that:

(a)   VAT is charged at a single fixed rate on both input VAT and output VAT

(b)   the amount due to HMRC is charged at a fixed rate on the total supplies for each VAT period

(c)   output VAT is charged at a fixed rate and input VAT is charged at a lower rate

(d)   VAT invoices must show the fixed rate charged by HMRC for the supplies made

Which **ONE** of these options is correct?

3.10 The cash accounting scheme:

(a) is normally operated in conjunction with the flat rate scheme

(b) allows for VAT to be paid by monthly instalments

(c) allows businesses to account for VAT on the basis of the date of payments received

(d) requires a supplier to submit a VAT Return once every twelve months

Which **ONE** of these options is correct?

3.11 State which of the three VAT Special Schemes each of the statements set out below relates to. Choose out of:

– Annual Accounting Scheme

– Cash Accounting Scheme

– Flat Rate Scheme

Write your answer in the box on the right (using the words annual, cash or flat).

(a)	this scheme will automatically provide for relief on any bad debt	
(b)	a supplier submits a VAT Return once every twelve months	
(c)	payment is charged at a percentage rate related to the type of business	
(d)	payment can be made in nine equal monthly instalments	
(e)	this scheme may be operated with the annual accounting scheme	
(f)	the VAT Return is due two months after the VAT period	
(g)	this scheme accounts for output VAT on the date payment is received	
(h)	this scheme does not have to record every single VAT transaction	

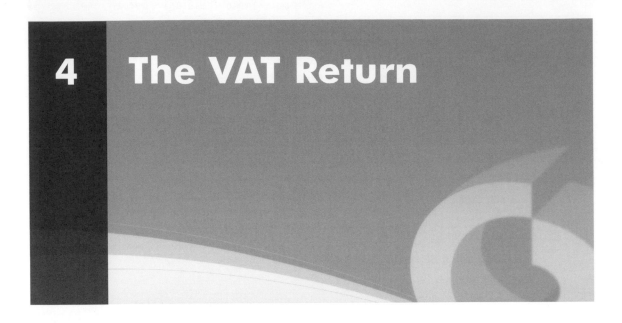

4 The VAT Return

this chapter covers...

This chapter describes how a business prepares the VAT Return – the form on which:

■ the output tax and input tax for the VAT period are summarised

■ the amount due to (or from) HM Revenue & Customs is calculated

This chapter describes:

■ the documents a business needs to keep for recording transactions involving VAT

■ the accounting records involving VAT which are needed to provide the figures for the VAT Return

■ the central role played by the VAT Control Account

■ how to deal with any EU acquisitions made during the VAT period

■ how to adjust for the VAT content of any bad debts incurred by the business – ie amounts which include output VAT that have been billed to customers, but are never likely to be paid

■ how to adjust when too much input VAT has been claimed back in error on a previous VAT Return

■ how to adjust when too little output tax has been paid to HMRC in error on a previous VAT Return

Lastly, the chapter explains:

■ how the appropriate figures are entered onto the VAT Return and how it is submitted online to HMRC

■ the time limits involved in submitting a VAT Return and the penalties that are payable if it is submitted late

KEEPING VAT RECORDS

VAT and VAT records

The accounting system of a VAT-registered business should record:

- input tax on purchases and expenses
- output tax on sales

It must be appreciated that accounting systems vary substantially from business to business, but the basic principles will remain the same: data has to be collected periodically (normally quarterly) so that input tax can be set off against output tax for the completion of the VAT Return.

It is important to have a working knowledge of the records that have to be maintained by a VAT-registered business. They are set out in the 'What records must I keep?' section of the online VAT Guide at www.hmrc.gov.uk. The basic records that relate specifically to VAT include:

- **copies of sales invoices** (ideally in numerical/date order) – these are the tax invoices which set out the output tax charged (if it is charged). Businesses do not have to keep copies of simplified invoices for £250 or less including VAT
- **originals of purchase invoices** (ideally given a consecutive reference number) – these are the tax invoices which set out the input tax which the business can normally reclaim. No invoice is required for purchases from a coin operated telephone, vending machine, or for car parking or toll charges that have a gross value of £25 or less
- **credit notes** relating to adjustments made to sales and purchase invoices
- documentation relating to EU **acquisitions**
- a **VAT control account** – also known simply as a 'VAT Account' – which records or summarises all items of input and output tax and acts as the source of data for the VAT Return

other business records

The additional business records involving VAT that should be kept by the business include:

- bank statements, paying-in slips and cheque book stubs
- purchase orders and delivery notes
- cash books and petty cash books
- purchases and sales day books
- ledger accounts
- payroll records
- computer printouts and reports
- annual accounts

We will now look in more detail at the records needed for sales (output tax) and purchases and expenses (input tax). For the purposes of your studies we will look at a business that buys and sells on credit and maintains a manual accounting system. You should always bear in mind that there are other businesses that trade on cash terms (immediate payment) and which have computer accounting programs which automate many of the processes that we will be describing.

records for output tax (sales)

Records for output tax include:

sales day book

This lists sales made on credit and is compiled from sales invoices issued by the business. It normally has an analysis column for VAT which is totalled periodically and used in the output VAT calculation.

sales returns day book

Any credit given (eg for returned goods, adjustments for overcharges) may involve VAT and deduction should be made from output tax. A separate sales returns day book, with a VAT analysis column, will normally be kept by the business and will be compiled from credit notes and debit notes issued.

cash book – receipts side

This includes a VAT analysis column and records details of other receipts **not on credit** which involve output tax, eg cash sales. Receipts for credit sales customers should be ignored because the amounts received include VAT which has already been dealt with in the sales day book when the invoice was issued.

records for input tax (purchases and expenses)

Records for input tax include:

purchases day book

This lists all purchases made on credit and has an analysis column for VAT which is totalled periodically.

purchases returns day book

Any credit received (eg for returned goods, adjustments for overcharges) may involve VAT and deduction should be made from input tax. A separate purchases returns day book, with a VAT analysis column, will normally be kept by the business and will be compiled from credit notes and debit notes.

cash book – payments side

This lists expenses paid by the business; VAT **for non-credit items** should be taken from the cash book analysis column. VAT on payments for credit purchases should be ignored because the amounts paid out include VAT which has already been dealt with in the purchases day book when the invoice was received.

A **petty cash book** with a VAT column may also be used to list small expenses and will need to be accounted for in the VAT calculations.

VAT CONTROL ACCOUNT

The central record for any VAT-registered business's bookkeeping system is the **VAT control account** into which all input and output tax is entered. This is referred to in the HMRC VAT Guide as the 'VAT Account'.

The balance of the VAT control account represents the amount owing to (or due from) HM Revenue & Customs.

The illustration below is developed from the layout recommended by HM Revenue & Customs in the VAT Guide. It shows entries for a supplier that normally has a surplus of output tax over input tax, which means that the supplier pays VAT to HM Revenue & Customs. An illustration with sample figures and explanatory notes is shown on the next page.

VAT Control Account – summary of entries

VAT deductible (input tax)	VAT payable (output tax)
Purchases Day Book VAT monthly totals, *less* any credit notes received/debit notes issued	Sales Day Book VAT monthly totals, *less* any credit notes issued/debit notes received
Cash Book – items not in Purchases Day Book	Cash Book – items not in Sales Day Book
Petty Cash Book – VAT on small expenses	
VAT allowable on EU Acquisitions	VAT due on EU Acquisitions
Correction of error(s) from previous returns (not exceeding £10,000 net)	Correction of error(s) from previous returns (not exceeding £10,000 net)
Bad debt relief	
= TOTAL TAX DEDUCTIBLE	= TOTAL TAX PAYABLE
	less TOTAL TAX DEDUCTIBLE
	equals TAX PAYABLE ON VAT RETURN

You should note that the control account shown below is not a double-entry account in the strict sense; for example, items such as credit notes are deducted on each side rather than being entered on the opposite side. In practice the VAT control account will be maintained in whatever way the accounting system – manual or computerised – requires. The important point is that the entries used for the VAT Return are all accounted for in a consistent way.

Study the VAT control account below and read the notes on this and the next page.

VAT Control Account			
VAT deductible: input tax		**VAT payable: output tax**	
	£		£
Purchases Day Book £10,500.00		Sales Day Book £18,110.50	
less credit notes £175.00	10,325.00	*less* credit notes £275.00	17,835.50
Cash Book	750.00	Cash Book	960.50
Petty Cash Book	15.95		
EU Acquisitions	2,110.00	EU Acquisitions	2,110.00
Bad Debt relief	675.00	Correction of error	175.69
TOTAL INPUT TAX	13,875.95	TOTAL OUTPUT TAX	21,081.69
		less TOTAL INPUT TAX	13,875.95
		equals VAT DUE	7,205.74

input tax

This is shown on the left-hand (debit) side of the account. We will explain each of these items in turn.

Purchases Day Book
The figure of £10,500.00 is the total of the input VAT shown in the VAT analysis columns in the Purchases Day Book. The figure of £175 is the input VAT total of the Purchases Returns Day Book.

Cash Book
The figure of £750 is taken from the total of the VAT analysis column of the Cash Book (payments side).

Petty Cash Book
The figure of £15.95 is taken from the total of the VAT analysis column of the Petty Cash Book.

EU Acquisitions

EU Acquisitions are purchases made from another EU state. The figure of £2,110.00 is the VAT which is paid on the acquisition but is also treated as an allowable input tax deduction.

Bad debt relief

A **bad debt** is an amount owing which a supplier writes off in the books because the debt is unlikely ever to be paid off – the buyer may have 'gone bust' for example.

Bad debt relief is the VAT scheme in which HM Revenue & Customs allows a business to claim back VAT which it has charged to a customer and already paid to HMRC, and which it has no chance of recovering. Bad debt relief is available for debts which are more than six months and less than four years and six months old.

The debt must also have been written off in the supplier's accounts and transferred to a separate bad debt account.

Note that bad debt relief cannot be reclaimed when the cash accounting scheme is used.

output tax

This is shown on the right-hand (credit) side of the account. We will explain each of these items in turn.

Sales Day Book

The figure of £18,110.50 is the total of the output VAT shown in the VAT analysis columns in the Sales Day Book. The figure of £275 is the output VAT total of the Sales Returns Day Book.

Cash Book

The figure of £960.50 is taken from the total of the VAT analysis column of the Cash Book (receipts side).

EU Acquisitions

EU Acquisitions are purchases made from another EU state. The figure of £2,110.00 is the VAT which relates to the acquisition.

Correction of errors

In this case the business owes HMRC a net £175.69. This error could have been caused by:

■ the amount of input VAT included has been too high

■ the amount of output VAT included has been too low

Correction of errors is explained in more detail on the next page.

VAT due calculation

VAT due is calculated by deducting the total of the input VAT side from the total of the output VAT side:

£21,081.69 minus £13,875.95 equals £7,205.74

VAT Account reconciliation with the VAT Return

The calculation in the VAT control account of VAT due to HM Revenue & Customs shown on the previous page should always agree with the total payment calculated on the VAT Return (see page 69). This is an important internal check for any VAT-registered business.

Note also that if the total input VAT in the VAT control account (left-hand side) is greater than the total output VAT (right-hand side), this means that the business will reclaim VAT from HMRC. The appropriate calculation will therefore be shown in the VAT control account on the left-hand side. This would regularly happen in the case of a business which produced zero-rated goods: VAT would be charged at 0% (ie no output VAT to account for) but allowable input VAT on purchases and expenses could all be reclaimed.

net errors of £10,000 or less

You will have seen that the output VAT side of the VAT control account on page 64 includes an error correction of £175.69. This correction is effectively adding this amount of output VAT to what is due for the VAT period.

HM Revenue & Customs allows businesses to correct **net errors** made in previous VAT periods of £10,000 or less (or 1% of quarterly turnover, subject to a maximum of £50,000) in later VAT Returns through the VAT control account.

Net error is the difference between the total of errors in output tax and the total of the errors in input tax. In the majority of cases, hopefully, there will only be one error, and this will be the 'net error'. Typical errors include failure to charge output tax on chargeable supplies, charging at the wrong rate, or arithmetical errors in the accounts.

If the error is over the £10,000 limit, or over 1% of quarterly turnover, subject to a maximum of £50,000, the matter will need to be reported to HM Revenue & Customs as a 'voluntary disclosure' (see page 76).

treatment of VAT paid and reclaimed

One omission from the VAT control account on page 64 is the VAT actually paid or reclaimed **for the previous VAT period**. Most businesses which sell standard-rated supplies will pay the VAT surplus to HM Revenue & Customs; other businesses – eg bookshops – which sell zero-rated supplies, will end up paying more VAT on inputs than they charge on outputs, and so will normally be able reclaim VAT from HM Revenue & Customs each time they submit a VAT Return.

The reason the entries are not shown in the VAT control account is that they cancel each other out and so have **no effect on the VAT due or owing** at the end of the period.

At the beginning of each VAT period the VAT control account will have an opening balance, either

- VAT due to be paid to HM Revenue & Customs – shown on the right-hand side of the account as a credit balance brought forward (this is the figure at the bottom of the account on page 64), or

- VAT reclaimable from HM Revenue & Customs – which will be shown on the left-hand side as a debit balance brought forward

When the VAT payment is made by the supplier (or received, if VAT is reclaimable) during the VAT period, the opening balance will be cancelled out. The net effect of the two entries on the account balance will be nil.

The examples below show how VAT paid and reclaimed is treated:

VAT payable by supplier

VAT CONTROL ACCOUNT (extract)

VAT deductible (input tax)	£	VAT payable (output tax)	£
Bank	12,400	Balance brought forward	12,400
(VAT paid by supplier)		(previous period's VAT due to be paid by supplier)	

VAT reclaimable by supplier

VAT CONTROL ACCOUNT (extract)

VAT deductible (input tax)	£	VAT payable (output tax)	£
Balance brought forward	10,000	Bank	10,000
(previous period's VAT reclaimable by supplier)		(VAT received by supplier from HM Revenue & Customs)	

THE VAT RETURN – ONLINE SUBMISSION

When the VAT figures have been transferred to the VAT control account and the amount of VAT due or reclaimable has been calculated, the VAT Return can then be completed. Nearly all businesses must do this by online submission at www.hmrc.gov.uk.

A sample online VAT Return is shown on the next page, and a Case Study follows on pages 72-75. The boxes are completed as follows:

1   The total VAT due on sales and other outputs. This total should be adjusted for any credit notes issued and errors (£10,000 net or less) on previous returns.

2   VAT due on acquisitions from other EU states.

3   The total of boxes 1 and 2. This is calculated automatically and in real time by HMRC.

4   The total VAT reclaimed on purchases and other inputs (less any credit notes). This total includes tax on acquisition of goods from other EU states and errors (£10,000 net or less) on previous returns.

5   This is box 3 minus box 4, and is automatically calculated online when the figures are input in boxes 3 and 4. If the figure in box 5 is positive, this is the amount payable to HM Revenue & Customs. If the figure in box 5 is negative, this amount in box 5 will be repaid to the supplier submitting the form.

6   The total of sales and other outputs excluding any VAT. This will include exempt, standard and zero-rated supplies and supplies to EU and non-EU states. Remember to adjust the total for any credit notes/debit notes.

7   The total of purchases (inputs) excluding any VAT. This includes standard, zero and exempt supplies, imports and acquisitions from EU states. Remember to adjust the total for any credit notes/debit notes.

8   The total of supplies of goods and related services, excluding VAT, to EU states (note that 'related services' refers to items such as freight and insurance charges for the goods).

9   The total of acquisition of goods and related services, excluding VAT, from EU states (as above, 'related services' refers to items such as freight and insurance charges for the goods).

Enter VAT return figures ⑦

Please enter your figures in the boxes below then click the 'Next' button to continue. For further information on how to complete your return please follow the link <u>Filling in your VAT Return</u>

Completing your return is different if you use the Flat Rate Scheme. Further information can be found by following the link <u>Flat Rate Scheme for small businesses.</u>

The 'Total VAT due (Box 3)' and 'Net VAT to be paid to HMRC or reclaimed by you (Box 5)' figures will be automatically calculated and displayed after you click the 'Next' button.

Please note: The system will time out if you do not use it for 15 minutes. You can save a draft return by clicking the 'Save draft return' button, but please remember to complete and submit the return by the due date.

Please note: Enter values in pounds sterling, including pence, for example 1000.00.

* indicates required information

VAT due in this period on **sales** and other outputs (Box 1):* [   ]
⑦

VAT due in this period on **acquisitions** from other **EC Member*** [   ]
States (Box 2): ⑦

Total VAT due **(the sum of boxes 1 and 2)** (Box 3):   **Calculated value**

VAT reclaimed in this period on **purchases** and other inputs,* [   ]
(including acquisitions from the EC) (Box 4): ⑦

Net VAT to be paid to HM Revenue & Customs or reclaimed by   **Calculated value**
you **(Difference between boxes 3 and 4)** (Box 5):

Total value of **sales** and all other outputs excluding any VAT.* [   ]
Include your box 8 figure (Box 6): ⑦
Whole pounds only

Total value of **purchases** and all other inputs excluding any* [   ]
VAT. **Include your box 9 figure** (Box 7): ⑦
Whole pounds only

Total value of all **supplies** of goods and related costs, excluding* [   ]
any VAT, to other **EC Member States** (Box 8): ⑦
Whole pounds only

Total value of all **acquisitions** of goods and related costs,* [   ]
excluding any VAT, from other **EC Member States** (Box 9): ⑦
Whole pounds only

If you want to save a draft copy of this return, please click the 'Save draft return' button below, alternatively click 'Next' to continue to submit your VAT return.

(Back)   (Save draft return)   (Next)

electronic payments to HMRC

As we have already seen in Chapter 4, nearly all businesses must now submit online VAT Returns. If an electronic VAT Return has been submitted any VAT payable must be paid electronically. HMRC recommends that this is done by direct debit, however businesses can also pay electronically using online or telephone banking, online credit or debit cards, BACs or CHAPS. The method of payment used by a business will affect the date on which the payment must be made. There is a handy tool on the HMRC website entitled 'VAT payment deadline calculator' which will tell you the appropriate payment date depending on the method that you use. Go to www.hmrc.gov.uk and search for 'VAT payment deadline calculator'.

electronic repayment by HMRC

In the same way that there are rules governing the timing of method of payment for VAT due to HMRC there are also obligations imposed on HMRC if the net VAT in Box 5 of the VAT return is a repayment due to the business. Where this is the case HMRC are obliged to schedule electronic repayment into the business's bank account. This will normally be within 10 working days but may take up to 21 days if HMRC has a query. Certain circumstances may mean that a repayment of VAT is not made automatically, for example if there is an outstanding amount owed to HMRC by the business.

THE PAPER-BASED VAT RETURN – FORM VAT 100

The paper-based VAT Return is now only permitted in exceptional circumstances.

The relevant parts of the VAT 100 form which need to be completed are shown on the opposite page. The boxes are dealt with in the same way as an online submission detailed on pages 68-69.

notes on completion of VAT 100

- if a VAT payment is being enclosed, the relevant box should be ticked
- the form should be signed by an authorised person
- the form should be returned by the due date in the envelope provided (normally one month after the end of the VAT period)
- do not leave any boxes blank – enter 'none' if there is no figure to insert
- always have the arithmetic and figures checked
- mistakes should be crossed through and correct figures inserted; the amendments should be initialled

PAPER-BASED VALUE ADDED TAX RETURN (extract)

		£	p
VAT due in this period on sales and other outputs	**1**	3655	20
VAT due in this period on acquisitions from other EC Member States	**2**	490	00
Total VAT due (the sum of boxes 1 and 2)	**3**	4145	20
VAT reclaimed in this period on purchases and other inputs (including acquisitions from the EC)	**4**	3652	00
Net VAT to be paid to Customs or reclaimed by you (Difference between boxes 3 and 4)	**5**	493	20
Total value of sales and all other outputs excluding any VAT. Include your box 8 figure.	**6**	20726	00
Total value of purchases and all other inputs excluding any VAT. Include your box 9 figure.	**7**	18260	00
Total value of all supplies of goods and related services, excluding any VAT, to other EC Member States.	**8**	NONE	00
Total value of all acquisitions of goods and related services, excluding any VAT, from other EC Member States.	**9**	2800	00

If you are enclosing a payment, please tick this box

✔

DECLARATION: You, or someone on your behalf, must sign below.

I, _JAMES ELROY FLETCHER_ — declare that the
(Full name of signatory in BLOCK LETTERS)

information given above is true and complete.

Signature _J E Fletcher_   Date 9 July 20 14

A false declaration can result in prosecution

FANCY THAT LTD – COMPLETING THE VAT RETURN

situation

Fancy That Limited is a wholesaler of fancy goods – gifts and cards – which are supplied on credit terms to shops in the UK, although a small proportion is sold for cash. Most of the goods are sourced in the UK, but some are imported from Italy and Spain.

Fancy That Limited is VAT-registered and its VAT quarters run from January to March, April to June, July to September and October to December. Most of the goods sold are standard-rated, but a few stock lines – mainly books – are zero-rated.

As the annual turnover of Fancy That Ltd is over £100,000, the VAT Return is submitted online.

It is now the first week in April. The data for the January-March VAT Return has been compiled. You have been asked to complete the VAT Control Account and prepare the online VAT 100 ready for input and authorisation by Dan Brookshaw, Finance Director.

The data is taken from the manual accounting system and summarised as follows:

SALES DAY BOOK SUMMARY			
	Zero-rated sales	**Standard-rated sales**	**VAT**	**Total sales (standard-rated)**
	£	£	£	£
January	2,930.50	15,170.15	3,034.03	18,204.18
February	1,923.81	21,689.03	4,337.80	26,026.83
March	2,706.61	22,729.50	4,545.90	27,275.40
TOTAL	7,560.92	59,588.68	11,917.73	71,506.41

PURCHASES DAY BOOK SUMMARY			
	Zero-rated purchases	**Standard-rated purchases**	**VAT**	**Total purchases (standard-rated)**
	£	£	£	£
January	00.00	8,791.60	1,758.32	10,549.92
February	00.00	12,326.50	2,465.30	14,791.80
March	00.00	9,731.95	1,946.39	11,678.34
TOTAL	00.00	30,850.05	6,170.01	37,020.06

CASH BOOKS – NON CREDIT ITEMS			
	NET £	VAT £	GROSS £
from main cash book			
Cash sales (Jan-Mar)	4,926.80	985.36	5,912.16
Cash purchases (Jan-Mar)	3,500.00	700.00	4,200.00
from petty cash book			
Expenses (Jan-Mar)	456.90	91.38	548.28

Additional information:

- Fancy That's purchases and expenses in the period in question are all standard-rated.

- EU acquisitions for the period totalled £17,794.03, VAT due is £3,558.80.

- The business has issued the following sales credit notes to its customers:
  £491.50 + £98.30 VAT = £589.80

- The business has received the following credit notes from its suppliers:
  £579.21 + £115.84 VAT = £695.05

- In January Fancy That paid VAT of £4,106.52 for the last quarter to HM Revenue & Customs; as the amount cancelled out the balance brought down in VAT Control Account, it is ignored for the purposes of the current period VAT calculations.

- The account of Furbo Ltd, a customer, has been written off as a bad debt. Bad debt relief of £48.00 may be claimed on the VAT Return.

- The accounts office made an error on a VAT calculation on an invoice during the last VAT quarter: a customer has been undercharged £75.29 output tax. Fortunately he has agreed to accept an invoice for this amount (he can reclaim it as input tax anyway). The problem for you is that the last quarter's VAT Return was £75.29 short on output tax. This error needs correcting on the current VAT Return.

solution

The data will be entered in the VAT Control Account in order to calculate the amount of VAT due to HM Revenue & Customs. The summary shown at the top of the next page is not the way the ledger account will actually appear in the double-entry system of the business, but it is displayed here in summary form to make the entries clearer.

The VAT Control Account Summary shows:

- totals for input tax and output tax – and the source of the figures

- the calculation for the VAT due to HM Revenue & Customs for the period

When the VAT Control Account has been checked, the figures can then be used to work out the totals for the VAT 100 form – see the calculations that follow the account summary. The data that will be entered on the VAT 100 are shown here with a grey background. The first five boxes involve VAT amounts and work out the total amount due to HM Revenue & Customs. Note that pence are omitted in boxes 6, 7 and 9.

VAT Control Account – summary of entries

VAT deductible: input tax		VAT payable: output tax	
	£		£
Purchases Day Book £6,170.01		Sales Day Book £11,917.73	
less credit notes £115.84	6,054.17	*less* credit notes £98.30	11,819.43
Cash Book	700.00	Cash Book	985.36
Petty Cash Book	91.38		
EU Acquisitions	3,558.80	EU Acquisitions	3,558.80
Bad debt relief	48.00	Correction of error	75.29
TOTAL INPUT TAX	10,452.35	TOTAL OUTPUT TAX	16,438.88
		less TOTAL INPUT TAX	10,452.35
		equals VAT DUE	5,986.53

data entered in the VAT Return

			£	£
Box 1	Sales Day Book (adjusted for credit notes)	11,819.43		
	Correction of error	75.29		
	Cash sales	985.36		
			12,880.08	
Box 2	EU Acquisitions		3,558.80	
Box 3	Box 1 plus Box 2 - automatically calculated online*		16,438.88	
Box 4	Purchases Day Book (less credit notes)	6.054.17		
	Cash book	700.00		
	Petty cash book	91.38		
	EU Acquisitions	3,558.80		
	Bad debt relief	48.00		
			10,452.35	
Box 5	Net VAT due (box 3 less box 4) - automatically calculated*		5,986.53	

Boxes 6 to 9 deal with sales/purchases before VAT. Note that pence are omitted.

			£	£
Box 6	Zero-rated credit sales	7,560.92		
	Standard-rated credit sales	59,588.68		
	less credit notes	(491.50)		
	Cash sales	4,926.80		
			71,584.90	
Box 7	Purchases on credit	30,850.05		
	less credit notes	(579.21)		
	Cash book	3,500.00		
	Petty cash	456.90		
	EU Acquisitions	17,794.03		
			52,021.77	

Box 8   £0.00

Box 9   EU Acquisitions: £17,794.03

* Note that because the VAT Return is submitted online Boxes 3 and 5 will be calculated automatically and will not need to be input. They are shown here for information purposes.

Note also that the balance of the VAT Control Account agrees with (reconciles with) the amount of VAT that is due to be paid to HM Revenue & Customs shown on the VAT Return in Box 5. This amount is £5,986.53.

VAT return figures

VAT due in this period on **sales** and other outputs (Box 1):	**£12880.08**
VAT due in this period on **acquisitions** from other **EC Member States** (Box 2):	**£3558.80**
Total VAT due **(the sum of boxes 1 and 2)** (Box 3):	**£16438.88**
VAT reclaimed in this period on **purchases** and other inputs, (including acquisitions from the EC) (Box 4):	**£10452.35**
Net VAT to be paid to HM Revenue & Customs or reclaimed by you **(Difference between boxes 3 and 4)** (Box 5):	**£5986.53**
Total value of **sales** and all other outputs excluding any VAT. **Include your box 8 figure** (Box 6):	**£71,584.00**
Total value of **purchases** and all other inputs excluding any VAT. **Include your box 9 figure** (Box 7):	**£52021.00**
Total value of all **supplies** of goods and related costs, excluding any VAT, to other **EC Member States** (Box 8):	**£0.00**
Total value of all **acquisitions** of goods and related costs, excluding any VAT, from other **EC Member States** (Box 9):	**£17,794.00**

Declaration

When you submit the above information, you are making a legal declaration that the information is correct and complete to the best of your knowledge and belief. A false declaration can result in prosecution.

(Back)   (Submit)

DEADLINES, PENALTIES AND ERROR REPORTING

deadlines for submission

It is important that a business submits the VAT Return and makes payment of VAT due so that HM Revenue & Customs receives it by the due date.

If a business submits its VAT Return **online**, the due date is normally a month and seven calendar days after the end of the VAT period when payment is made electronically. The annual accounting scheme is an exception to this rule, allowing a two month period for submission of the VAT Return.

surcharges for late VAT Returns and VAT payments

A business must submit its VAT Return and pay any VAT by the due date. If HM Revenue & Customs receives the VAT Return or VAT payment after the due date, the business is 'in default' and may have to pay a surcharge in addition to the VAT owed. The first time a business defaults, it will be sent a warning known as a **Surcharge Liability Notice** which states that if the business pays late again during the following 12 months – known as the surcharge period – the business may have to pay a surcharge. This **default surcharge** is a percentage of the unpaid VAT, which initially will be 2% of the unpaid VAT. If the business continues to make late payments it will be charged increasing penalties of 5%, 10% and 15% of the unpaid VAT. It is important that a business realises that failure to pay VAT due or penalties that are imposed is a criminal offence and can result in prosecution.

net errors over the limit – voluntary disclosure

We have already seen that some errors in previous VAT Returns can be corrected in the current VAT Return. If, however, there should be a net error of more than £10,000 (or over 1% of quarterly turnover, subject to a maximum of £50,000), this should be advised to the local VAT Office on Form VAT 652 or in a letter as a **voluntary disclosure**. The details that will need to be disclosed are:

- the amount(s)
- the VAT period in which the error occurred
- whether the errors involved input or output tax (or both)
- whether the error was in favour of the business or HMRC

It should be noted that businesses can use a form VAT 652 to report errors of any size, even those below the error reporting threshold.

Failure to disclose errors, however innocent they may be, can have serious consequences. A HM Revenue & Customs investigation could result in a **misdeclaration penalty**, which could mean a 15% charge on unpaid VAT. No misdeclaration penalty can be charged if a voluntary disclosure is made.

Chapter Summary

- It is important that a business maintains accurate and comprehensive accounting records, keeping the records for at least six years. They may be needed for inspection by HM Revenue & Customs.

- VAT records that must be kept include:
  - copies of sales invoices
  - originals of purchase invoices
  - credit notes issued and received
  - VAT control account
  - other associated records

- VAT-registered businesses may use manual or computerised accounting systems. The normal sources of accounting data for the completion of the VAT Return are:
  - sales and purchases day books, and returns day books (for credit items)
  - cash book and petty cash book (for non-credit items)

- This data is compiled in a VAT control account as follows:

VAT Control Account – summary of entries

VAT deductible (input tax)	VAT payable (output tax)
Purchases Day Book VAT monthly totals, *less* any credit notes received/debit notes issued	Sales Day Book VAT monthly totals, *less* credit notes issued/debit notes received
Cash Book – items not in Purchases Day Book	Cash Book – items not in Sales Day Book
Petty Cash Book – VAT on small expenses	
VAT allowable on EU Acquisitions	VAT due on EU Acquisitions
Correction of error(s) from previous returns (not exceeding £10,000 net)	Correction of error(s) from previous returns (not exceeding £10,000 net)
Bad debt relief	
= TOTAL TAX DEDUCTIBLE	= TOTAL TAX PAYABLE
	less TOTAL TAX DEDUCTIBLE
	equals TAX PAYABLE ON VAT RETURN

- In addition the VAT control account will record VAT owing and paid to HM Revenue & Customs (or VAT owed and paid by HM Revenue & Customs) – but payments are not entered on the VAT Return.

- The VAT control account may also be used to make adjustments for small errors (under £10,000) on previous VAT Returns and for Bad Debt Relief which will reimburse for output VAT charged on a debt which has been written off.

- Most VAT Returns and payments (if required) are submitted online by the payment date indicated by the computer. This date is normally a month and seven days after the end of the VAT period when payment is made electronically. This process should be approved by an authorised person.

- The paper-based VAT Return and cheque payment (if required) should be completed and despatched within the timescale allowed (normally a month from the end of the VAT period); the VAT 100 should be signed by an authorised person.

- Net VAT errors of £10,000 or less (or 1% of quarterly turnover, subject to a £50,000 maximum limit) can be corrected on a subsequent VAT Return. Errors over these limits should be advised as a 'voluntary disclosure' to HM Revenue & Customs in a letter or on Form VAT 652.

- If a VAT Return is not returned within the stipulated timescale, HM Revenue & Customs will issue a twelve month surcharge liability notice; a further default within the twelve months may result in a default surcharge.

<table>
<tr><td rowspan="8">**Key Terms**</td></tr>
<tr><td>**VAT Control Account**</td><td>a central account which collects all the accounting data needed for the VAT Return; it is not a double-entry account in the strict sense but more of a collection point for data for the VAT Return</td></tr>
<tr><td>**bad debt relief**</td><td>a scheme available for any registered supplier whereby output VAT paid over to HM Revenue & Customs on a debt which has subsequently (over 6 months after the due date) gone bad, is reclaimable through the VAT Return</td></tr>
<tr><td>**VAT Return**</td><td>Form VAT 100 is completed online or in paper format by VAT-registered suppliers at the end of each VAT period in order to calculate the amount of VAT due to HM Revenue & Customs or reclaimable from them</td></tr>
<tr><td>**voluntary disclosure**</td><td>disclosure of a net error (over set limits) in VAT calculations to HM Revenue & Customs by a registered supplier</td></tr>
<tr><td>**misdeclaration penalty**</td><td>a penalty imposed on a VAT-registered supplier who is found by HM Revenue & Customs to have errors and irregularities in the VAT records</td></tr>
<tr><td>**surcharge liability notice**</td><td>a notice issued by HM Revenue & Customs to a VAT-registered supplier who has failed to make a VAT Return within the stipulated period</td></tr>
<tr><td>**default surcharge**</td><td>a percentage charge on an amount of unpaid VAT</td></tr>
</table>

Activities

4.1 A business can use the following records as a source of information for **input VAT** to include in the VAT Control Account:

(a) sales day book, cash book (payments side), petty cash book (payments)

(b) purchases day book, cash book (payments side), petty cash book (payments)

(c) purchases day book, cash book (receipts side), purchases returns day book

(d) sales day book, cash book (payments side), purchases returns day book

Which **ONE** of these options is correct?

4.2 A business can use the following records as a source of information for **output VAT** to include in the VAT Control Account:

(a) sales day book, cash book (receipts side), petty cash book (payments)

(b) purchases day book, cash book (payments side), purchases returns day book

(c) sales day book, cash book (payments side), purchases returns day book

(d) sales day book, cash book (receipts side), sales returns day book

Which **ONE** of these options is correct?

4.3 Businesses must keep copies of invoices for all purchases except where they relate to:

(a) car parking charges of £50 or less including VAT

(b) car parking charges of £50 or less excluding VAT

(c) car parking charges of £25 or less including VAT

(d) car parking charges of £25 or less excluding VAT

Which **ONE** of these options is correct?

4.4 A business that has overclaimed input tax of £120 in error on the last VAT Return should:

(a) add it to the input tax side of the VAT Control Account as an error correction

(b) deduct it from the Sales Day Book monthly VAT total in the VAT Control Account

(c) deduct it from the input tax side of the VAT Control Account as an error correction

(d) add it to the Bad Debt Relief figure in the VAT Control Account

Which **ONE** of these options is correct?

4.5 A business has written off a customer account as a bad debt. The written-off amount included VAT of £48 which has been accounted for in the last VAT Return. This amount should be

(a) included as Bad Debt Relief on the input tax side of the VAT Control Account

(b) included as Bad Debt Relief on the output tax side of the VAT Control Account

(c) included as a credit note to be deducted on the output tax side of the VAT Control Account

(d) included as a credit note to be deducted on the input tax side of the VAT Control Account

Which **ONE** of these options is correct?

4.6 **You are to** construct VAT control accounts from the VAT figures shown below. The figures have been extracted from the accounting records of four different businesses. In each case ensure that you calculate the VAT due or reclaimable for the VAT period. Note: any VAT payable or reclaimable for the previous period is to be ignored.

VAT FIGURES	Business A	Business B	Business C	Business D
	£	£	£	£
Purchases Day Book	2,720.00	3,239.50	5,726.05	3,923.50
Sales Day Book	5,961.70	5,906.33	9,176.23	521.30
Credit notes received	326.50	107.60	195.50	170.90
Credit notes issued	501.29	321.90	391.80	81.25
Cash book purchases (non-credit)	275.60	179.29	173.76	1,256.81
Cash book sales (non-credit)	329.73	260.75	356.25	723.80
Petty cash book purchases	13.85	nil	18.92	41.20
EU Acquisitions	796.30	78.00	1,523.90	nil
VAT overpaid previous period	nil	nil	271.20	17.50
VAT underpaid previous period	nil	32.65	86.30	nil
Bad debt relief	nil	85.50	89.23	29.50

The format shown below can be used to set up the VAT Control Account. You will need to calculate the final amount of VAT due or reclaimable. If the final total is reclaimable it should be shown in brackets.

VAT deductible (input tax)	VAT payable (output tax)
Purchases Day Book VAT total, *less* any credit notes received/ debit notes issued	Sales Day Book VAT total, *less* any credit notes issued/debit notes received
Cash Book – items not in Purchases Day Book	Cash Book – items not in Sales Day Book
Petty Cash Book – VAT on small expenses	
Acquisitions from EU states	Acquisitions from EU states
Corrections of errors from previous periods (not exceeding £10,000 net)	Corrections of errors from previous periods (not exceeding £10,000 net)
Bad debt relief	
= TOTAL TAX DEDUCTIBLE	= TOTAL TAX PAYABLE
	less TOTAL TAX DEDUCTIBLE
	equals TAX PAYABLE/(RECLAIMABLE)

4.7 You work as an assistant in a firm of accountants and have been asked to draw up VAT Returns for four clients. You have extracted the relevant data from their accounting records and have set it out on a spreadsheet shown below.

You are to calculate the totals for all nine boxes of the four VAT Returns ready for checking. If you wish, you can use the table set out on the next page for entering the figures.

	Business 1	Business 2	Business 3	Business 4
	£	£	£	£
VAT FIGURES EXTRACTED				
Sales day book	12,684.77	19,635.27	3,653.00	3,927.15
Credit notes issued	243.57	793.02	62.43	112.39
Cash sales	1,586.40	347.76	785.07	345.31
Purchases day book	7,197.52	12,350.16	1,262.57	11,618.66
Credit notes received	174.14	421.56	32.58	215.36
Cash purchases	367.79	1,159.66	60.00	nil
Petty cash expenses	nil	104.20	38.19	55.16
Bad debt relief	639.80	850.00	nil	250.00
Overpayment (previous period)*	nil	258.92	nil	365.12
Underpayment (previous period)**	nil	nil	95.20	109.90
EU acquisitions	nil	3,750.04	247.21	10,047.96
NET SALES AND RECEIPTS				
Zero-rated sales	126.75	8,326.18	1,507.29	75,800.00
Standard-rated sales	63,423.86	98,176.35	18,265.00	19,635.75
Credit notes issued	1,217.85	3,965.10	312.18	561.95
Cash sales (standard-rated)	7,932.01	1,738.81	3,925.37	1,726.58
Zero-rated purchases	1,290.00	3,706.70	295.80	2,560.22
Standard-rated credit purchases	35,987.60	61,750.80	6,312.87	58,093.30
Credit notes received	870.72	2,107.83	162.91	1,076.84
Cash payments (standard-rated)	1,838.96	5,798.32	300.00	nil
Petty cash expenses	nil	521.00	190.95	275.81
EU acquisitions	nil	18,750.21	1,236.09	50,239.80

Suggested answer layout for 4.7:

VAT Return Box No.	Business 1	Business 2	Business 3	Business 4
1				
2				
3				
4				
5				
6				
7				
8				
9				

Notes on data on previous page – overpayment and underpayment of VAT in previous period

* Overpayment of VAT (previous period) relates to input VAT not included in the last VAT Return.

** Underpayment of VAT (previous period) relates to output VAT not included in the last VAT Return.

4.8 You work for J M Talbot Limited as an accounts assistant and are required to collect the data for the quarterly online VAT Return and then input it ready for authorisation.

The following figures have been extracted from the company's accounting records:

UK Sales		
Date		£
31 Jan 20-3	Sales day book	195,000.00
28 Feb 20-3	Sales day book	200,000.00
31 Mar 20-3	Sales day book	210,000.00

Sales to EC states		
Date		£
31 Jan 20-3	Sales day book	25,000.00
28 Feb 20-3	Sales day book	36,500.00
31 Mar 20-3	Sales day book	97,000.00

UK Purchases		
Date		£
31 Jan 20-3	Purchases day book	120,000.00
28 Feb 20-3	Purchases day book	98,000.00
31 Mar 20-3	Purchases day book	105,000.00

VAT: output tax		
Date		£
31 Jan 20-3	Sales day book	39,000.00
28 Feb 20-3	Sales day book	40,000.00
31 Mar 20-3	Sales day book	42,000.00

VAT: input tax		
Date		£
31 Jan 20-3	Purchases day book	24,000.00
28 Feb 20-3	Purchases day book	19,600.00
31 Mar 20-3	Purchases day book	21,000.00

Additional information:

- There are no credit notes involved.
- There are no imports from or exports to non-EC states.
- You are advised that in the last VAT Return the amount of input tax claimed had been overstated by £120.00. You have been asked to adjust for this error.
- You are also advised that Bad Debt Relief of £135.00 can be claimed in this VAT Return
- The date is 8 April 20-3.
- The current VAT rate is 20%.

You are to:

(a) Calculate the total input VAT and total output VAT for the VAT quarter, making the appropriate calculations and adjustments.

(b) Calculate the amount of VAT due to (or due from) HM Revenue & Customs.

(c) Complete boxes 1 to 9 of the VAT Return (shown below) for the quarter ended 31 March 20-3.

		£	p
VAT due in this period on sales and other outputs	**1**		
VAT due in this period on acquisitions from other EC Member States	**2**		
Total VAT due (the sum of boxes 1 and 2)	**3**		
VAT reclaimed in this period on purchases and other inputs (including acquisitions from the EC)	**4**		
Net VAT to be paid to Customs or reclaimed by you (Difference between boxes 3 and 4)	**5**		
Total value of sales and all other outputs excluding any VAT. Include your box 8 figure.	**6**		**00**
Total value of purchases and all other inputs excluding any VAT. Include your box 9 figure.	**7**		**00**
Total value of all supplies of goods and related services, excluding any VAT, to other EC Member States.	**8**		**00**
Total value of all acquisitions of goods and related services, excluding any VAT, from other EC Member States.	**9**		**00**

5   VAT communications

this chapter covers...

This chapter describes the situations where it is necessary to be able to communicate information about VAT:

- *to the managers and staff of a business*
- *to HM Revenue & Customs*

The areas in which VAT information must be communicated internally within the business include:

- *informing managers about the way in which payment of VAT by the business to HM Revenue & Customs will affect the cashflow and financial forecasts of the business*
- *informing managers and staff about what happens when the rate of VAT changes on a certain date and how this affects operations such as invoicing*
- *informing managers and staff about other changes in VAT legislation such as:*
    - *a change in the limit for reporting of errors on a previous VAT Return*
    - *a change in the way in which a special scheme operates*

Lastly, this chapter describes the way in which a business communicates with HM Revenue & Customs, for example asking advice about a certain area of VAT legislation which needs clarification.

VAT AND THE CASH FLOW OF A BUSINESS

the timing of VAT payments

The timing of VAT payments can have a significant effect on the cash flow of a business.

Normally a VAT-registered business will complete a VAT Return every three months online. The VAT Return will have to be submitted and payment made electronically by one month and seven days after the end of the VAT period. If the customers of the business pay their invoices promptly the business will be able to bank the cheques – which include output VAT charged – and use this money as 'working capital' until it has to be paid to HM Revenue & Customs when the VAT Return is due.

Suppose, for example:

■ a consignment of goods is invoiced in mid-January

■ the invoice is paid in mid-February and the money is banked

■ the VAT quarter runs from 1 January to 31 March

■ the VAT Return and payment are due by 7 May

The business will then have the use of the VAT money due for at least two and a half months until the VAT payment is made in the first week of May. The time line looks like this:

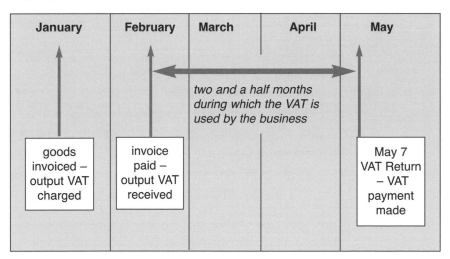

If this happened every VAT quarter, the business would receive a regular and useful boost to its working capital.

the effect on the cash budget

The situation described on the previous page would also be reflected in the company's cash budget, which would show:

- the output VAT charged to trade receivables (debtors) as part of the regular **monthly** cash inflow
- the **quarterly** payments to HM Revenue & Customs as cash outflows in May, August, November and February
- the increased bank balance which results from the lag in making the quarterly payments to HM Revenue & Customs

further improvements to cash flow – some emails

In the email shown below, Tariq, an accounts supervisor, suggests to John Turner, his manager, that even tighter credit control would further improve the company's cash flow.

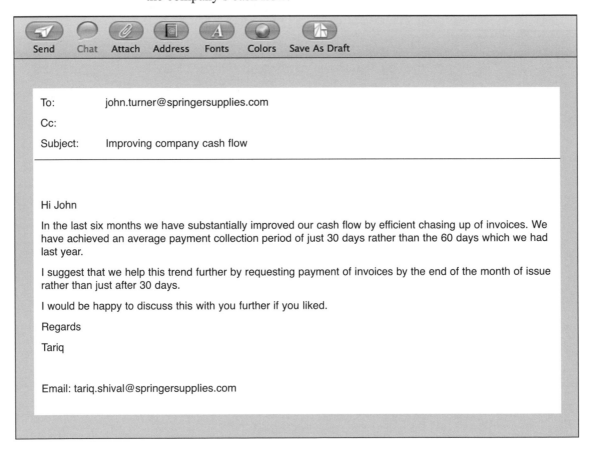

Send   Chat   Attach   Address   Fonts   Colors   Save As Draft

To: john.turner@springersupplies.com

Cc:

Subject: Improving company cash flow

Hi John

In the last six months we have substantially improved our cash flow by efficient chasing up of invoices. We have achieved an average payment collection period of just 30 days rather than the 60 days which we had last year.

I suggest that we help this trend further by requesting payment of invoices by the end of the month of issue rather than just after 30 days.

I would be happy to discuss this with you further if you liked.

Regards

Tariq

Email: tariq.shival@springersupplies.com

John Turner then replies as follows:

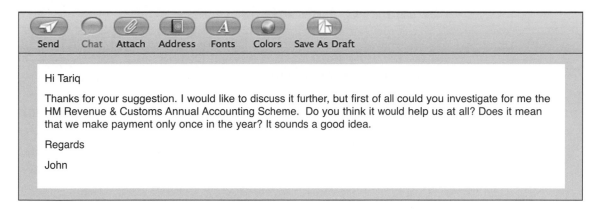

Tariq then looks into this and finds that the idea is not such a good one because payments have to be made more than once a year. He replies as follows:

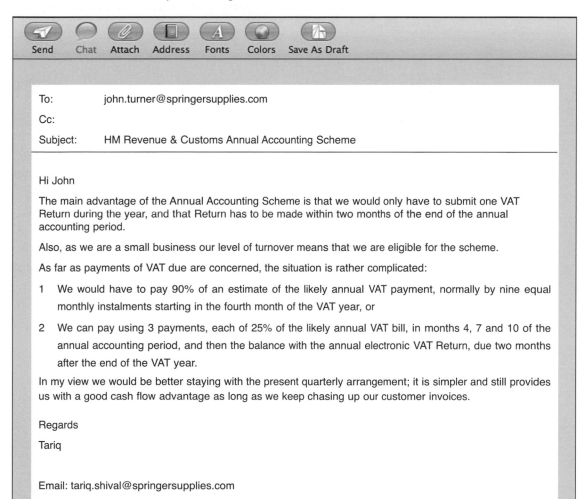

VAT and cash flow – conclusion

The exchange of emails on the last two pages shows how VAT information can be effectively communicated between members of a business team. In this case the points covered include:

- the cash flow advantage of having money in the bank because payment to HM Revenue & Customs is made over a month after the end of the VAT period – and sales invoices are settled promptly some months before

- the features of the annual accounting scheme for VAT which involves the annual submission of the VAT Return, but complex arrangements for payment of the VAT due to HM Revenue & Customs during the year

VAT LEGISLATION

what is VAT law?

The law affects businesses by setting out principles which dictate what the businesses should or should not do in their everyday dealings.

In the case of VAT law these principles originate from a number of different sources:

- **VAT Directives** of the European Economic Community – the Directive 2006/112/EC, amended in 2010, is the most important of these

- the **Value Added Tax Act 1994** passed by the UK Parliament and amended from time-to-time in the various **Finance Acts** which turn Budget measures into legal requirements

- UK **statutory instruments** – these are detailed rules and regulations which have the authority of Acts of Parliament, but do not have to go through the lengthy processes required for passing an Act of Parliament

- certain **VAT Notices** published by HM Revenue & Customs and available on www.hmrc.gov.uk

As you can see, finding your way around VAT law can be rather complicated. HM Revenue & Customs, however, can normally provide the answer to most legal queries relating to VAT.

changes in VAT regulations

It is an unfortunate fact that VAT regulations change frequently, most importantly in the period following the Budget. VAT rates are also subject to variation from time-to-time.

All these changes have significant effects on the running of businesses, for example:

- **rate changes** affect the calculation of output VAT and the total prices on invoices, credit notes, price lists and price stickers on goods; a rate change and its timing will also affect claims for input tax

- changes in the **types of goods and services that are chargeable to VAT** and the rates charged, for example the extension of reduced rate VAT to child car seats and domestic fuel

- the introduction of new **VAT special schemes** and the modification of the upper turnover limit on existing schemes may affect how a business accounts for VAT

When there are changes to VAT legislation or regulation, specific timescales for the changes to be applied must be adhered to.

In this chapter we describe how a business deals with these changes and communicates the necessary information to the right people.

CHANGING THE VAT RATE

The most common and far-reaching change to the VAT system is a change in VAT rate. Zero rate by definition will not vary and, at the time of writing, the reduced rate VAT has been 5% for a number of years. Standard rate VAT, however, is subject to change, and when it does change it affects the great majority of businesses.

The normal reason for a change is Government policy which may need to:

- increase or decrease consumer spending in the economy – an increase, for example, will discourage spending

- increase tax revenue for the Government – an increase in VAT rate will help to fund Government spending

For businesses, however, the changes brought about by a change in VAT rate will be more immediate. Whether the accounting system is kept manually or on computer, the basic principles remain the same.

DEALING WITH AN INCREASE IN THE STANDARD VAT RATE

Suppose the UK Government announced an increase in standard rate VAT by 2% to take effect on 1 April.

This means that for any sales of standard-rated goods or services made on or after 1 April a business must charge VAT at the increased rate. This change only applies to the standard VAT rate. There are no changes to sales that are zero-rated or reduced-rated for VAT. There are also no changes to VAT-exempt supplies.

How does this affect businesses?

retailers

If the business is a **retailer** it must use the increased rate for all takings received on or after 1 April. If the customer paid after 1 April for something taken away or delivered before 1 April, the sale took place before 1 April and the lower rate should be used.

businesses that sell on credit

If the business issues **VAT invoices**, it must use the increased rate for all VAT invoices issued on or after 1 April. If a business provided goods or services before 1 April and issued a VAT invoice after that date a business can choose to account for VAT at the lower rate.

special rules for services

If a business provides **services** that started **before** 1 April but finished them **afterwards** it may invoice for the work done up to 31 March at the lower rate and the remainder at the higher rate.

continuous supplies of services

If a business provides **continuous services** such as the leasing of office equipment, it should account for the VAT due whenever it issues an invoice or receives payment, whichever is the earlier, ie it should charge at the higher rate after 1 April, the date of the increase.

reclaiming input VAT

Businesses should claim back the VAT charged by its suppliers in the normal way. Invoices received after the rate change relating to purchases made before the rate change should show VAT at the lower rate: this is the amount that should be reclaimed.

VAT rate changes and special schemes

If a business operates a special VAT scheme, it may be affected by a change in VAT rate, for example:

■ a business that uses the **Cash Accounting Scheme** (based on when payments are received) will need to identify sales made before the date the change was made, eg 1 April, and charge them the lower rate

■ a business that uses the **Flat Rate Scheme** (payments due to HMRC based on a flat percentage – not the VAT rate) will need to use the revised percentage announced by HM Revenue & Customs for use after the change in standard rate

If a business uses the **Annual Accounting Scheme**, there will be no change in the payment of instalments to HM Revenue & Customs.

who needs to know about a VAT rate rise?

A change in the rate of VAT should always be announced by HM Revenue & Customs well in advance. A business will not only need to notify its own staff, it will also need to notify its customers well in advance.

advising the customers

If the customers of a shop, for example, know about a rise in the VAT rate in advance, they will be motivated to buy more before the rate rise as they will obviously pay less.

Advance notices in shops about a rate rise are therefore a 'must'; they will encourage sales before the rise and also avoid the inevitable confusion and annoyance of customers when the price paid for goods does increase.

As you might imagine, the motor trade does well before a VAT rate rise because a person buying a car may be able to save a large amount of money by paying the lower rate of VAT before the rate rise.

advising the staff

When a VAT rate change is announced by the Government all businesses should make plans well in advance to make sure:

- employees know about the change
- the necessary adjustments are made to manual and computerised systems.

The areas of a business that will particularly need to know about the changes are:

- accounting staff dealing with **day-to-day transactions involving VAT**, eg invoicing and purchasing

- accounting staff dealing with drawing up **financial forecasts**, eg the cash budget – a rise in output VAT charged will increase monthly inflows of cash and will also affect the monthly outflow when the VAT is paid to HM Revenue & Customs

- marketing, sales and customer services staff who draw up and advise about **price lists**, both in printed form and also web-based

- shop floor and warehouse staff who deal with **pricing goods**, either with price stickers or bar codes

A business is likely to have an action plan on file ready for a rate change and will be able to send out in advance suitable notices and emails. An example of a Memorandum (which will be emailed to all management staff) is shown on the next page. The situation here is an increase in standard rate VAT from 20% to 22.5% on 4 January.

MEMORANDUM

To: All Departmental Managers

From   Alex Rowlands, Finance Director

Subject: Increase in standard rate VAT from 20% to 22.5% w.e.f. 4 January

---

As you will know, standard rate VAT is due to increase from 20% to 22.5% on 4 January.

It is essential that you all carry out the necessary procedures to ensure that the changeover goes smoothly and that our customers are aware of the price changes. I would like to highlight a number of key areas to you:

1 Accounts Department: Sales and Purchases Ledger should ensure that the settings on the computerised accounting system for VAT on invoices and credit notes are amended to 22.5%.

2 Accounts Department: Management Accounting Section should ensure that the spreadsheets for cash budgets are amended to show the increase in output VAT received.

3 Marketing and Sales: all publicity literature quoting VAT-inclusive prices should be withdrawn before 4 January and revised prices calculated and quoted on new publicity material. The website should be similarly checked for prices and the VAT rate on the online shop amended accordingly from 4 January.

4 Warehouse and shop: any price stickers or barcodes on stock showing pre-increase prices should be removed and replaced by new price stickers and barcodes.

Please ensure that in each case detailed instructions are issued to your staff. These instructions are available as standing instructions in the Company Procedures Manual.

Regards

Alex Rowlands

OTHER AMENDMENTS TO VAT SCHEMES

Although the alteration in the rate of VAT is probably the most common change a business will have to deal with in relation to VAT, there are other areas of change which will need to be communicated to staff by employers. These include:

the reporting of errors on previous VAT Returns

As we have seen already (on page 76), HM Revenue & Customs allows corrections on VAT Returns for net errors in the calculation of input and output VAT up to a limit of £10,000 (at the time of writing). This may be subject to change in the future. Should this happen in the future, the management of the business would have to communicate the amount of the revised limit to the relevant staff, probably by email, so that the employees responsible for the compilation and authorisation of the VAT Return would comply with the new requirements.

a change related to a special scheme

As we have already seen in Chapter 3, HM Revenue & Customs has introduced a number of special VAT schemes to help businesses – especially smaller businesses – deal with the administration of VAT in a cost-effective way. These include:

■ the **Cash Accounting Scheme**, which is based on accounting for VAT when payments are received and made, rather than when invoices are received and issued

■ the **Flat Rate Scheme**, where payments due to HMRC are based on a flat percentage related to the trade in which the business operates

■ the **Annual Accounting Scheme** which only requires a VAT Return to be made every twelve months and involves payment of VAT by regular instalments

These schemes are subject to modification from time-to-time. For example:

■ the turnover limit which applies to certain schemes may be raised

■ the flat rate percentage which applies to the flat rate scheme may be adjusted when the standard VAT rate changes

In each case the person in charge of VAT administration in the business must communicate the details to the relevant staff. In some cases the business may want to review whether it is worth staying with the special scheme. In other cases, if the annual turnover of the business exceeds the limit applicable to the special scheme, the business may have to withdraw from the scheme. All these factors will need to be communicated within the business and, where necessary, form the basis for internal discussion and possibly also for consultation with the accountants of the business.

COMMUNICATING WITH HM REVENUE & CUSTOMS

Businesses may from time-to-time need to contact HM Revenue & Customs to ask advice about certain issues, for example whether they should charge VAT on a certain transaction, or are uncertain about the rate of VAT.

There have been some interesting cases in the past which have become national news, for example whether a certain well-known brand of orange and chocolate food product is classified as a biscuit or cake (zero-rated) or, because it is chocolate-covered, VAT should be chargeable. The answer in this case was that it was a 'cake' and therefore zero-rated. Most queries are less in the public eye than this and can be readily answered by the various channels of communication provided to businesses and their advisors by HM Revenue & Customs, who can be contacted:

- through online services
- by telephone
- by email
- by post

The channel of communication will vary depending on the nature of the enquiry.

online information

The HM Revenue & Customs **website** – www.hmrc.gov.uk – is a rich source of information with a powerful search facility. This website will provide the information to answer many queries which a business may raise, for example:

'Can you give me details of special schemes?'

'What is the definition of a tax point?'

'What goods and services are VAT-exempt?'

Many businesses complete their VAT Return online and so will be registered for the HM Revenue & Customs Online Services, which are accessible with a User ID and Password. These services include a useful **Online Services Helpdesk**.

telephone advice

If a business is unable to find the answer to its question on the HMRC website, the quickest and easiest way of obtaining information is to **telephone** the VAT helpline where most VAT questions can be answered. The number is obtainable from www.hmrc.gov.uk.

emailed enquiries

A business may also email enquiries to HM Revenue & Customs. Email communication can be rather restrictive because if a business emails a question to HMRC and wants an email reply, it must state in the email that it understands and accepts the security risks of sending personal information electronically. If HMRC's reply needs to contain any personal or confidential information, the reply will have to be made by letter or telephone. It may, in fact, be easier to send the enquiry by post (see next page).

writing to HM Revenue & Customs

If a business is having problems finding out the answers to its enquiries online or by telephone, the traditional and effective method of communication is to write a letter and send it by post.

A letter can be used when:

- the business has referred to the VAT information published by HMRC on its website or in printed form and and cannot find a satisfactory answer
- the business is in real doubt about how VAT affects a particular transaction and getting a decision is financially important for the business and its customer
- the telephone helpline has asked the business to write a letter

When a business writes to HM Revenue & Customs, it will need to provide certain information:

- the VAT Registration Number
- the full postal address and telephone number
- an explanation of the problem and why the business cannot make a decision about it
- full details of the situation or transaction

The following information should also be provided so that HM Revenue & Customs can get a full view of the situation and will be in a position to respond more quickly.

- is the business the supplier or the buyer?
- is the customer registered for VAT?
- does the query relate to goods or to services?
- are any countries other than the UK involved and will goods be supplied to them?
- if services are involved, what sort are they?

Normally a letter will be written, signed and sent by an authorised employee within the business – a manager, for example. The usual letter writing skills should be used:

- the letter should be clearly and simply expressed, using the correct terminology for areas relating to VAT
- the letter should be complete – all the necessary details should be present (see above)
- accuracy – all figures and any calculations should be correct and carefully checked

Then it will be a matter of waiting to hear what HM Revenue & Customs have to say and taking the appropriate action.

■ The timing of VAT payments to HM Revenue & Customs can affect the cash flow position of a business. Cash flow can be improved if payment of customer invoices (which include output VAT) is made in advance of the payment of net VAT due to HM Revenue & Customs.

■ Email is an efficient way of communicating information about VAT between individuals and departments within a business.

■ VAT law is derived from a number of different sources:
  – EC Directives
  – UK statute law and statutory instruments
  – VAT Notices published by HM Revenue & Customs

■ Changes in VAT regulations affect businesses in a variety of ways and so businesses must keep up-to-date with:
  – rate changes
  – changes to the types of goods and services subject to VAT
  – changes to special schemes

■ Businesses must communicate in an appropriate way to the right people the actions that should be taken to deal with the changes to VAT.

■ Businesses can communicate with HM Revenue & Customs in a variety of ways: online research and enquiries, telephone, email and letter.

EU Directives   the legal framework created by the European Union for the drafting of laws within the individual European states

Finance Act   the UK Act of Parliament passed each year to put into effect changes proposed in the Budgets

Act of Parliament   UK statute passed by both Houses of Parliament which becomes the law enforceable within the UK

Statutory Instrument   subsidiary rules and regulations which have the force of law and the authority of Parliament

VAT Notices   regulations imposed by HM Revenue & Customs which have legal force

Online Services   the online interface of HMRC which provides advice and enables businesses to submit VAT Returns online

Activities

5.1   The cash flow of a business which makes quarterly payments of net VAT to HMRC will improve if:

(a)   the business switches to the VAT annual accounting scheme

(b)   the business reduces the credit period on its sales invoices from 60 to 30 days of invoice

(c)   the business pays its suppliers' purchase invoices after 30 days rather than 60 days

(d)   the business goes over to online VAT Return submission and payment

Which **ONE** of these options is correct?

5.2   Suppose that the Budget, supported by subsequent legislation, states that from 1 January the standard rate of VAT will increase from 20% to 22.5%.

You run a business selling fashion clothes which are standard-rated for VAT.

Answer the following questions:

(a)   This increase in VAT will encourage people to buy clothes after January 1. True or False?

(b)   A customer receiving clothes before 1 January and paying for the goods after 1 January will pay VAT at the lower rate of VAT. True or False?

5.3   You work in the accounts department of a business and have received an email from your manager telling you that a 2.5% VAT standard rate decrease will come into effect from 1 October. The date today is 1 September.

Complete the gaps in the text of the email using the following words:

20%	*output*	*credit notes*	*22.5%*	*cash budget*	*decrease*

As you will know, standard rate VAT is due to [   ] from 22.5% to 20% on 1 October.

It is essential that you all carry out the necessary procedures to ensure that the changeover goes smoothly.

You will need to make sure that:

1   The settings on the computerised accounts system for VAT on invoices and [   ] are amended to [   ]

2   All price lists showing VAT at [   ] should be amended to show the lower rate as soon as possible.

3   The [   ] spreadsheets should be amended to show a lower amount of [   ] VAT received on sales invoices.

Answers to activities

CHAPTER 1: INTRODUCTION TO VALUE ADDED TAX

1.1   (b)

1.2   (a)

1.3   (b)

1.4   (a)

1.5   (d)

1.6   (d)

1.7   (c)

1.8   (b)

1.9   (a)

1.10   (d)

1.11   (b)

1.12   (d)

CHAPTER 2: VAT AND BUSINESS DOCUMENTS

2.1   (c)

2.2   (b)

2.3   (a)

2.4   (d)

2.5   No VAT registration number, no VAT rates or amounts listed. Not a valid VAT receipt.

2.6   (c)

2.7   (b)

2.8   (a)

2.9   (c)

2.10   (b)

2.11   (b)

2.12   (a)

CHAPTER 3: INPUTS AND OUTPUTS AND SPECIAL SCHEMES

3.1   (b)

3.2   (c)

3.3   (a)

3.4   (d)

3.5   (d)

3.6   (c)

3.7   (d)

3.8   (a)

3.9   (b)

3.10   (c)

3.11

(a)	this scheme will automatically provide for relief on any bad debt	cash
(b)	a supplier submits a VAT Return once every twelve months	annual
(c)	payment is charged at a percentage rate related to the type of business	flat
(d)	payment can be made in nine equal monthly instalments	annual
(e)	this scheme may be operated with the annual accounting scheme	flat or cash
(f)	the VAT Return is due two months after the VAT period	annual
(g)	this scheme accounts for output VAT on the date payment is received	cash
(h)	this scheme does not have to record every single VAT transaction	flat

CHAPTER 4: THE VAT RETURN

4.1 (b)

4.2 (d)

4.3 (c)

4.4 (c)

4.5 (a)

4.6

VAT Control Account – Business A			
VAT deductible: input tax	£	**VAT payable: output tax**	£
Purchases Day Book £2,720.00 *less* credit notes £326.50	2,393.50	Sales Day Book £5,961.70 *less* credit notes £501.29	5,460.41
Cash Book	275.60	Cash Book	329.73
Petty Cash Book	13.85		
EU Acquisitions	796.30	EU Acquisitions	796.30
TOTAL INPUT TAX	3,479.25	TOTAL OUTPUT TAX	6,586.44
		less TOTAL INPUT TAX	3,479.25
		equals VAT DUE	3,107.19

VAT Control Account – Business B			
VAT deductible: input tax	£	**VAT payable: output tax**	£
Purchases Day Book £3,239.50 *less* credit notes £107.60	3,131.90	Sales Day Book £5,906.33 *less* credit notes £321.90	5,584.43
Cash Book	179.29	Cash Book	260.75
EU Acquisitions	78.00	EU Acquisitions	78.00
Bad debt relief	85.50	Underpayment (previous period)	32.65
TOTAL INPUT TAX	3,474.69	TOTAL OUTPUT TAX	5,955.83
		less TOTAL INPUT TAX	3,474.69
		equals VAT DUE	2,481.14

VAT Control Account – Business C

VAT deductible: input tax	£	VAT payable: output tax	£
Purchases Day Book £5,726.05 *less* credit notes £195.50	5,530.55	Sales Day Book £9,176.23 *less* credit notes £391.80	8,784.43
Cash Book	173.76	Cash Book	356.25
Petty cash book purchases	18.92		
EU Acquisitions	1,523.90	EU Acquisitions	1,523.90
Bad debt relief	89.23		
Net overpayment (previous period)	184.90		
TOTAL INPUT TAX	7,521.26	TOTAL OUTPUT TAX	10,664.58
		less TOTAL INPUT TAX	7,521.26
		equals VAT DUE	3,143.32

VAT Control Account – Business D

VAT deductible: input tax	£	VAT payable: output tax	£
Purchases Day Book £3,923.50 *less* credit notes £170.90	3,752.60	Sales Day Book £521.30 *less* credit notes £81.25	440.05
Cash Book	1,256.81	Cash Book	723.80
Petty cash book purchases	41.20		
Bad debt relief	29.50		
Overpayment (previous period)	17.50		
TOTAL INPUT TAX	5,097.61	TOTAL OUTPUT TAX	1,163.85
		less TOTAL INPUT TAX	5,097.61
		equals VAT RECLAIMABLE	(3,933.76)

4.7

VAT Return Box No.	Business 1	Business 2	Business 3	Business 4
1	14,027.60	19,190.01	4,470.84	4,160.07
2	none	3,750.04	247.21	10,047.96
3	14,027.60	22,940.05	4,718.05	14,208.03
4	8,030.97	18,051.42	1,575.39	22,011.64
5	5,996.63	4,888.63	3,142.66	(7,803.61)
6	70,264	104,276	23,385	96,600
7	38,245	88,419	8,172	110,092
8	none	none	none	none
9	none	18,750	1,236	50,239

4.8

		£	p
VAT due in this period on sales and other outputs	**1**	121000	00
VAT due in this period on acquisitions from other EC Member States	**2**	0	00
Total VAT due (the sum of boxes 1 and 2)	**3**	121000	00
VAT reclaimed in this period on purchases and other inputs (including acquisitions from the EC)	**4**	64615	00
Net VAT to be paid to Customs or reclaimed by you (Difference between boxes 3 and 4)	**5**	56385	00
Total value of sales and all other outputs excluding any VAT. Include your box 8 figure.	**6**	763500	**00**
Total value of purchases and all other inputs excluding any VAT. Include your box 9 figure.	**7**	323000	**00**
Total value of all supplies of goods and related services, excluding any VAT, to other EC Member States.	**8**	158500	**00**
Total value of all acquisitions of goods and related services, excluding any VAT, from other EC Member States.	**9**	NONE	**00**

Workings for Box 4:	£
Input tax as per day book	64,600.00
Deduct overclaim of input tax (correction)	(120.00)
Add Bad Debt Relief	135.00
Box 4 total	64,615.00

CHAPTER 5: VAT COMMUNICATIONS

5.1   (b)

5.2   **(a)** = False

(b) = True

5.3

> As you will know, standard rate VAT is due to **decrease** from 22.5% to 20% on 1 October.
>
> It is essential that you all carry out the necessary procedures to ensure that the changeover goes smoothly.
>
> You will need to make sure that:
>
> 1 The settings on the computerised accounts system for VAT on invoices and **credit notes** are amended to **20%**.
>
> 2 All price lists showing VAT at **22.5%** should be amended to show the lower rate as soon as possible.
>
> 3 The **cash budget** spreadsheets should be amended to show a lower amount of **output** VAT received on sales invoices.

Reference Material

for AAT Assessment of Indirect Tax

For assessments from 1 January 2015 - 31 December 2015

Note: this reference material is accessible by candidates during their live computer based assessment for Indirect Tax.

INTRODUCTION

This document comprises data that you may need to consult during your Indirect Tax computer-based assessment.

The material can be consulted during the sample and live assessments through pop-up windows. It is made available here so you can familiarise yourself with the content before the test.

Do not take a print of this document into the exam room with you*.

This document may be changed to reflect periodical updates in the computer-based assessment, so please check you have the most recent version while studying. This version is based on Finance Act 2014 and is for use in AAT assessments 1 January – 31 December 2015.

Unless you need a printed version as part of reasonable adjustments for particular needs, in which case you must discuss this with your tutor at least six weeks before the assessment date.

INTRODUCTION TO VAT

VAT is a tax that's charged on most goods and services that VAT-registered businesses provide in the UK. It's also charged on goods and some services that are imported from countries outside the European Union (EU), and brought into the UK from other EU countries.

VAT is charged when a VAT-registered business sells taxable goods and services to either another business or to a non-business customer. This is called output tax.

When a VAT-registered business buys taxable goods or services for business use it can generally reclaim the VAT it has paid. This is called input tax.

Her Majesty's Revenue & Customs (HMRC) is the government department responsible for operating the VAT system. Payments of VAT collected are made by VAT-registered businesses to HMRC.

RATES OF VAT

There are three rates of VAT, depending on the goods or services the business provides. The rates are:

- standard – 20%. The standard-rate VAT fraction is 20/120 or 1/6

- reduced – 5%. The reduced rate VAT fraction is 5/105

- zero – 0%

There are also some goods and services that are:

- exempt from VAT

- outside the scope of VAT (outside the UK VAT system altogether)

Taxable supplies

Zero-rated goods and services count as taxable supplies and are part of taxable turnover, but no VAT is added to the selling price because the VAT rate is 0%.

If the business sells goods and services that are exempt, no VAT is added as they're not taxable supplies and they're also not taxable turnover.

Generally, a business can't register for VAT or reclaim the VAT on purchases if it only sells exempt goods and services. Where some of its supplies are of exempt goods and services, the business is referred to as partially exempt. It may not be able to reclaim the VAT on all of its purchases.

A business which buys and sells only – or mainly – zero-rated goods or services can apply to HMRC to be exempt from registering for VAT. This could make sense if the business pays little or no VAT on purchases.

Taxable turnover

Taxable turnover (or taxable outputs) consists of total standard rated sales plus all zero-rated sales but excludes exempt and out of scope sales.

REGISTRATION AND DEREGISTRATION LIMITS

Registration threshold

If, as at the end of any month, taxable turnover for the previous 12 months is more than the current registration threshold of £81,000, the business must register for VAT within 30 days. Registration without delay is required if, at any time, the value of taxable turnover in the next 30 day period alone is expected to be more than the registration threshold.

If trading is below the registration threshold

If taxable turnover hasn't crossed the registration threshold, the business can still apply to register for VAT voluntarily.

Deregistration threshold

The deregistration threshold is £79,000. If taxable turnover for the year is less than or equal to £79,000, or if it is expected to fall to £79,000 or less in the next 12 months, the business can either:

*   stay registered for VAT, or

*   ask for its VAT registration to be cancelled

KEEPING BUSINESS RECORDS AND VAT RECORDS

All VAT registered businesses must keep certain business and VAT records.

These records are not required to be kept in a set way, provided they:

*   are complete and up to date

*   allow the correct amount of VAT owed to HMRC or by HMRC to be worked out

*   are easily accessible when an HMRC visit takes place, eg the figures used to fill in the VAT Return must be easy to find

Business records

Business records which must be kept include the following:

*   annual accounts, including income statements

*   bank statements and paying-in slips

*   cash books and other account books

*   orders and delivery notes

*   purchase and sales books

*   records of daily takings such as till rolls

*   relevant business correspondence

In addition to these business records, VAT records and a VAT account must be kept.

VAT records

In general, the business must keep the following VAT records:

- Records of all the standard-rated, reduced rate, zero-rated and exempt goods and services that are bought and sold.

- Copies of all sales invoices issued. However, businesses do not have to keep copies of any less detailed (simplified) VAT invoices for items under £250 including VAT

- All purchase invoices for items purchased for business purposes unless the gross value of the supply is £25 or less and the purchase was from a coin operated telephone or vending machine, or for car parking charges or tolls.

- All credit notes and debit notes received.

- Copies of all credit notes and debit notes issued.

- Records of any goods or services bought for which there is no VAT reclaim, such as business entertainment.

- Records of any goods exported.

- Any adjustments, such as corrections to the accounts or amended VAT invoices.

- A VAT account

For how long must VAT records be kept?

Generally all business records that are relevant for VAT must be kept for at least six years. If this causes serious problems in terms of storage or costs, then HMRC may allow some records to be kept for a shorter period.

Keeping a VAT account

A VAT account is the separate record that must be kept of the VAT charged on taxable sales (referred to as output tax or VAT payable) and the VAT paid on purchases (called input tax or VAT reclaimable). It provides the link between the business records and the VAT Return. A registered business needs to add up the VAT in the sales and purchases records and then transfer these totals to the VAT account, using separate headings for VAT payable and VAT reclaimable.

The VAT account can be kept in whatever way suits the business best, as long as it includes information about the VAT that it:

- owes on sales

- owes on acquisitions from other European Union (EU) countries

- owes following a correction or error adjustment

- can reclaim on business purchases

- can reclaim on acquisitions from other EU countries

- can reclaim following a correction or error adjustment

- is reclaiming via VAT bad debt relief

The business must also keep records of any adjustments that have been made, such as balancing payments for the annual accounting scheme for VAT.

Information from the VAT account can be used to complete the return at the end of each accounting period. VAT reclaimable is subtracted from the VAT payable, to give the net amount of VAT to pay to or reclaim from HMRC.

Unless it is using the cash accounting scheme, a business must pay the VAT charged on invoices to customers during the accounting period that relates to the return, even if those customers have not paid the invoices.

EXEMPT AND PARTLY-EXEMPT BUSINESSES

Exempt goods and services

There are some goods and services on which VAT is not charged.

Exempt supplies are not taxable for VAT, so sales of exempt goods and services are not included in taxable turnover for VAT purposes. If a registered business buys exempt items, there is no VAT to reclaim.

(This is different to zero-rated supplies. In both cases VAT is not added to the selling price, but zero-rated goods or services are taxable for VAT at 0%, and are included in taxable turnover.)

Businesses which only sell or supply exempt goods or services

A business which only supplies goods or services that are exempt from VAT is called an exempt business. It cannot register for VAT, so it won't be able to reclaim any input tax on business purchases.

(Again this is different to zero-rated supplies, as a business can reclaim the input tax on any purchases that relate to zero-rated sales. In addition, a business which sells mainly or only zero-rated items may apply for an exemption from VAT registration, but then it can't claim back any input tax.)

Reclaiming VAT in a partly exempt business

A business that is registered for VAT but that makes some exempt supplies is referred to as partly or partially, exempt.

Generally, such businesses won't be able to reclaim the input tax paid on purchases that relate to exempt supplies.

However if the amount of input tax incurred relating to exempt supplies is below a minimum 'de minimus' amount, input tax can be reclaimed in full.

If the amount of input tax incurred relating to exempt supplies is above the 'de minimus' amount, only the part of the input tax that related to non-exempt supplies can be reclaimed.

TAX POINTS

The time of supply, known as the 'tax point', is the date when a transaction takes place for VAT purposes. This date is not necessarily the date the supply physically takes place.

Generally, a registered business must pay or reclaim VAT in the (usually quarterly) VAT period, or tax period, in which the time of supply occurs, and it must use the correct rate of VAT in force on that date. This means knowing the time of supply/tax point for every transaction is important, as it must be put on the right VAT Return.

Time of supply (tax point) for goods and services

The time of supply for VAT purposes is defined as follows.

- For transactions where no VAT invoice is issued the time of supply is normally the date the supply takes place (as defined below).

- For transactions where there is a VAT invoice, the time of supply is normally the date the invoice is issued, even if this is after the date the supply took place (as defined below).

To issue a VAT invoice, it must be sent (by post, email etc) or given to the customer for them to keep. A tax point cannot be created simply by preparing an invoice.

However there are exceptions to these rules on time of supply, detailed below.

Date the supply takes place

For goods, the time when the goods are considered to be supplied for VAT purposes is the date when one of the following happens.

- The supplier sends the goods to the customer.

- The customer collects the goods from the supplier.

- The goods (which are not either sent or collected) are made available for the customer to use, for example if the supplier is assembling something on the customer's premises.

For services, the date when the services are supplied for VAT purposes is the date when the service is carried out and all the work – except invoicing – is finished.

Exceptions regarding time of supply (tax point)

The above general principles for working out the time of supply do not apply in the following situations:

- For transactions where a VAT invoice is issued or payment is received in advance of the date of supply, the time of supply is the date the invoice is issued or the payment is received, whichever is the earlier.

- If the supplier receives full payment before the date when the supply takes place and no VAT invoice has yet been issued, the time of supply is the date the payment is received.

- If the supplier receives part-payment before the date when the supply takes place, the time of supply becomes the date the part-payment is received but only for the amount of the part-payment (assuming no VAT invoice has been issued before this date – in which case the time of supply is the date the invoice is issued). The time of supply for the remainder will follow the normal rules – and might fall in a different VAT period, and so have to go onto a different VAT return.

- If the supplier issues a VAT invoice more than 14 days after the date when the supply took place, the time of supply will be the date the supply took place, and not the date the invoice is issued. However, if a supplier has genuine commercial difficulties in invoicing within 14 days of the supply taking place, they can contact HMRC to ask for permission to issue invoices later than 14 days and move the time of supply to this later date.

VAT INVOICES

To whom is a VAT invoice issued?

Whenever a VAT-registered business supplies taxable goods or services to another VAT-registered business, it must give the customer a VAT invoice.

A VAT-registered business is not required to issue a VAT invoice to a non-registered business or to a member of the public, but it must do so if requested.

What is a VAT invoice?

A VAT invoice shows certain VAT details of a supply of goods and services. It can be either in paper or electronic form.

A VAT-registered customer must have a valid VAT invoice from the supplier in order to claim back the VAT they have paid on the purchase for their business.

What is NOT a VAT invoice?

The following are NOT VAT invoices:
- pro-forma invoices
- invoices for only zero-rated or exempt supplies
- invoices that state 'this is not a tax invoice'
- statements
- delivery notes
- orders
- letters, emails or other correspondence

A registered business cannot reclaim the VAT it has paid on a purchase by using these documents as proof of payment.

What a VAT invoice must show

A VAT invoice must show:
- an invoice number which is unique and follows on from the number of the previous invoice – any spoiled or cancelled serially numbered invoice must be kept to show to a VAT officer at the next VAT inspection
- the seller's name or trading name, and address
- the seller's VAT registration number
- the invoice date
- the time of supply or tax point if this is different from the invoice date
- the customer's name or trading name, and address
- a description sufficient to identify the goods or services supplied to the customer

For each different type of item listed on the invoice, the business must show:
- the unit price or rate, excluding VAT
- the quantity of goods or the extent of the services
- the rate of VAT that applies to what's being sold
- the total amount payable, excluding VAT

- the rate of any cash or settlement discount
- the total amount of VAT charged

If the business issues a VAT invoice that includes zero-rated or exempt goods or services, it must:

- show clearly that there is no VAT payable on those goods or services
- show the total of those values separately

Rounding on VAT invoices

The total VAT payable on all goods and services shown on a VAT invoice may be rounded to a whole penny. Any fraction of a penny can be ignored. (This concession is not available to retailers.)

Time limits for issuing VAT invoices

There is a strict time limit on issuing VAT invoices. Normally a VAT invoice (to a VAT-registered customer) must be issued within 30 days of the date of supply of the goods or services – or, if the business was paid in advance, the date payment was received. This is so the customer can claim back the VAT on the supply, if they're entitled to do so.

Invoices can't be issued any later without permission from HMRC, except in a few limited circumstances.

A valid VAT invoice is needed to reclaim VAT

Even if the business is registered for VAT, it can normally only reclaim VAT on purchases if:

- they are for use in the business or for business purposes and
- a valid VAT invoice for the purchase is received and retained.

Only VAT-registered businesses can issue valid VAT invoices. A business cannot reclaim VAT on any goods or services that are purchased from a business that is not VAT-registered.

Where simplified (less detailed) VAT invoices can be issued

Simplified VAT invoices

If a registered business makes taxable supplies of goods or services for £250 or less including VAT, then when a customer asks for a VAT invoice, it can issue a simplified (less detailed) VAT invoice that only needs to show:

- the seller's name and address
- the seller's VAT registration number
- the time of supply (tax point)
- a description of the goods or services
- the total payable including VAT

Also, if the supply includes items at different VAT rates then for each different VAT rate, the simplified VAT invoice must also show the VAT rate applicable to the item

Exempt supplies must not be included on a simplified VAT invoice.

If the business accepts credit cards, then it can create a simplified invoice by adapting the sales voucher given to the cardholder when the sale is made. It must show the information described above.

There is no requirement to keep copies of any less detailed invoices issued.

Pro-forma invoices

If there is a need to issue a sales document for goods or services not supplied yet, the business can issue a 'pro-forma' invoice or a similar document as part of the offer to supply goods or services to customers.

A pro-forma invoice is not a VAT invoice, and it should be clearly marked with the words "This is not a VAT invoice".

If a potential customer accepts the goods or services offered to them and these are actually supplied, then a VAT invoice must be issued within the appropriate time limit.

If the business has been issued with a pro-forma invoice by a supplier it can't be used to claim back VAT on the purchase. A VAT invoice must be obtained from the supplier.

Advance payments and deposits

An advance payment, or deposit, is a proportion of the total selling price that a customer pays before they are supplied with goods or services. When a business asks for an advance payment, the tax point is whichever of the following happens first:

- the date a VAT invoice is issued for the advance payment
- the date the advance payment is received

The business must include the VAT on the advance payment on the VAT Return for the period when the tax point occurs.

If the customer pays the remaining balance before the goods are delivered or the services are performed, another tax point is created when whichever of the following happens first:

- a VAT invoice is issued for the balance
- payment of the balance is received

Include the VAT on the balance on the VAT return for the period when the tax point occurs.

Discounts on goods and services

If any goods or services are discounted, VAT is charged on the discounted price rather than the full price.

When a business makes an offer to a customer such as 'we will pay your VAT', VAT is actually payable to HMRC on the amount the customer would have paid on the discounted price, not the amount they have paid at the full price.

Prompt payment (settlement) discounts

If a VAT-registered business supplies broadcasting or telecommunications services and offers a discount for early payment, VAT must be charged on the consideration actually paid by the buyer. For all other supplies VAT is charged on the discounted price irrespective of the payment made by the buyer.

Returned goods, credit notes, debit notes and VAT

For a buyer who has received a VAT invoice

If goods are returned to the seller for a full or partial credit there are three options:

- return the invoice to the supplier and obtain a replacement invoice showing the proper amount of VAT due, if any
- obtain a credit note or supplementary VAT invoice from the supplier

- issue a debit note to the supplier

If the business issues a debit note or receives a credit note, it must:
- record this in the accounting records
- enter it on the next VAT Return, deducting the VAT on the credit or debit note from the amount of VAT which can be reclaimed

For a seller who has issued a VAT invoice

If goods are returned by a customer, there are again three options:
- cancel and recover the original invoice, and issue a replacement showing the correct amount of any VAT due, if any
- issue a credit note or supplementary VAT invoice to the customer
- obtain a debit note from the customer

If the business issues a credit note or receives a debit note, it must:
- record this in the accounting records
- enter it on the next VAT Return, deducting the VAT on the credit or debit note from the amount of VAT payable

ENTERTAINMENT EXPENSES

Business entertainment

Business entertainment is any form of free or subsidised entertainment or hospitality to non-employees, for example suppliers and customers. Generally a business cannot reclaim input VAT on business entertainment expenses. The exception is that input tax can be reclaimed in respect of entertaining overseas customers, but not UK or Isle of Man customers.

Employee expenses and entertainment

The business can, however, reclaim VAT on employee expenses and employee entertainment expenses if those expenses relate to travel and subsistence or where the entertainment applies only to employees.

When the entertainment is in respect of both employees and non-employees, the business can only reclaim VAT on the proportion of the expenses that is for employees.

VEHICLES AND MOTORING EXPENSES

VAT and vehicles

When it buys a car a registered business generally can't reclaim the VAT. There are some exceptions – for example, when the car is used mainly as one of the following:
- a taxi
- for driving instruction
- for self-drive hire

If the VAT on the original purchase price of a car bought new is not reclaimed, the business does not have to charge any VAT when it is sold. This is because the sale of the car is exempt for VAT purposes. If the business did reclaim the VAT when it bought the car new, VAT is chargeable when it comes to sell it.

VAT-registered businesses can generally reclaim the VAT when they buy a commercial vehicle such as a van, lorry or tractor.

Reclaiming VAT on road fuel

If the business pays for road fuel, it can deal with the VAT charged on the fuel in one of four ways:

- Reclaim all of the VAT. All of the fuel must be used only for business purposes.

- Reclaim all of the VAT and pay the appropriate fuel scale charge – this is a way of accounting for output tax on fuel that the business buys but that's then used for private motoring.

- Reclaim only the VAT that relates to fuel used for business mileage. Detailed records of business and private mileage must be kept.

- Don't reclaim any VAT. This can be a useful option if mileage is low and also if fuel is used for both business and private motoring. If the business chooses this option it must apply it to all vehicles including commercial vehicles.

TRANSACTIONS OUTSIDE THE UK

Exports, despatches, supplying goods abroad: charging VAT

If a business sells, supplies or transfers goods out of the UK to someone in another country it may need to charge VAT on them.

Generally speaking, the business can zero-rate supplies exported outside the European Union (EU), or sent to someone who's registered for VAT in another EU country, provided it follows strict rules, obtains and keeps the necessary evidence, and obeys all laws.

Goods supplied to another EU country are technically known as despatches rather than exports. The term 'exports' is reserved to describe sales to a country outside the EU.

VAT on sales to someone who is not VAT registered in another EU country

When a business supplies goods to someone in another EU country, and they're not registered for VAT in that country, it should normally charge VAT.

VAT on sales to someone who is VAT registered in another EU country

If, however goods are supplied to someone who is registered for VAT in the destination EU country, the business can zero-rate the supply for VAT purposes, provided it meets certain conditions.

VAT on exports of goods to non-EU countries

VAT is a tax charged on goods used in the European Union (EU), so if goods are exported outside the EU VAT isn't charged, the supply can be zero-rated.

Imports and purchases of goods from abroad: paying and reclaiming VAT

Generally speaking, VAT is payable on all purchases of goods that are bought from abroad at the same rate that would apply to the goods if bought in the UK. The business must tell HMRC about goods that it imports, and pay any VAT and duty that is due.

VAT on goods from EU countries

If a business is registered for VAT in the UK and buys goods from inside the EU, these are known as acquisitions rather than imports. Enter the value of the acquisition in Box 9 and Box 7 of the VAT Return and account for VAT in Box 2 of the VAT return using the same rate of VAT that would apply if the goods were supplied in the UK. This VAT is known as acquisition tax. The business can reclaim the acquisition tax as if the goods were bought in the UK by including the same figure in Box 4, subject to the normal VAT rules for reclaiming input tax.

VAT on imports of goods from non-EU countries

VAT may be charged on imports of goods bought from non-EU countries. The business can reclaim any VAT paid on the goods imported as input tax.

BAD DEBTS

When a business can reclaim VAT on bad debts

VAT that has been paid to HMRC and which it has not been received from the customer can be reclaimed as bad debt relief. The conditions are that:

- the debt is more than six months and less than four years and six months old
- the debt has been written off in the VAT account and transferred to a separate bad debt account
- the debt has not been sold or handed to a factoring company
- the business did not charge more than the normal selling price for the items

Bad debt relief cannot be reclaimed when the cash accounting scheme is used.

How to claim bad debt relief

If the business is entitled to claim bad debt relief, add the amount of VAT to be reclaimed to the amount of VAT being reclaimed on purchases (input tax) and put the total figure in Box 4 of the VAT return.

To work out how much bad debt relief can be claimed on a VAT-inclusive balance, the relevant VAT fraction is applied to the unpaid amount.

COMPLETING THE VAT RETURN, BOX BY BOX

Two forms of VAT Return exist: the online version, which is completed by the majority of VAT-registered businesses, and a paper form for the few businesses which are exempt from online filing.

The online VAT Return is completed as follows;

Box 1 – VAT due in this period on sales and other outputs

- This is the total amount of VAT charged on sales to customers. It also has to include VAT due to HMRC for other reasons, for example fuel scale charges.

Box 2 – VAT due in this period on acquisitions from other EU Member States

- VAT due, but not yet paid, on goods bought from other EU countries, and any services directly related to those goods (such as delivery charges). The business may be able to reclaim this amount, and if so it must be included in the total in Box 4.

Box 3 – Total VAT due (the sum of boxes 1 and 2)

Box 4 – VAT reclaimed in this period on purchases and other inputs (including acquisitions from the EC)

- This is the VAT charged on purchases for use in the business. It should also include:

    - VAT paid on imports from countries outside the EU

    - VAT due (but not yet paid) on goods from other EU countries, and any services directly related to those goods (such as delivery charges) - this is the figure in Box 2.

Box 5 – Net VAT to be paid to Customs or reclaimed by you (difference between boxes 3 and 4)

Box 6 – Total value of sales and all other outputs excluding any VAT, include your Box 8 figure.

- Enter the total figure for sales (excluding VAT) for the period, that is the sales on which the VAT entered in Box 1 was based. Additionally, also include:

    - any zero-rated and exempt sales or other supplies made

    - any amount entered in Box 8

    - exports from outside the EU.

The net amount of any credit notes issued, or debit notes received, is deducted.

Box 7 – Total value of purchases and all other inputs excluding any VAT. Include your Box 9 figure.

- Enter the total figure for purchases (excluding VAT) for the period, that is the purchases on which the VAT entered in Box 4 was based. Additionally, also include:

    - any zero-rated and exempt purchases

    - any amount entered in Box 9

    - imports from outside the EU.

Box 8 – Total value of all supplies of goods and related costs, excluding any VAT, to other EU Member States

- Enter the total value of goods supplied to another EU country and services related to those goods (such as delivery charges).

Box 9 – Total value of acquisitions of goods and related costs, excluding any VAT, from other EU Member States

- Enter the total value of goods received from VAT registered suppliers in another EU country and services related to those goods (such as delivery charges).

VAT PERIODS, SUBMITTING RETURNS AND PAYING VAT

VAT Returns for transactions to the end of the relevant VAT period must be submitted by the due date shown on the VAT Return. VAT due must also be paid by the due date.

What is a VAT period?

A VAT period is the period of time over which the business records VAT transactions in the VAT account for completion of the VAT Return. The VAT period is three months (a quarter) unless the annual accounting scheme is used. The end dates of a business's four VAT periods are determined when it first registers for VAT, but it can choose to amend the dates on which its VAT periods end. This is often done to match VAT periods to accounting period ends.

Submitting VAT Returns online and paying HMRC electronically

It is mandatory for virtually all VAT-registered traders to submit their VAT Returns to HMRC using online filing, and to pay HMRC electronically.

Due dates for submitting the VAT return and paying electronically

Businesses are responsible for calculating how much VAT they owe and for paying VAT so that the amount clears to HMRC's bank account on or before the due date. Paying on time avoids having to pay a surcharge.

The normal due date for submitting each VAT Return and electronically paying HMRC any VAT that is owed is one calendar month after the end of the relevant VAT period, unless the annual accounting scheme is operated. The normal due date for the return and payment can be found on the return.

Online filing and electronic payment mean that businesses get an extended due date for filing the return of up to seven extra calendar days after the normal due date shown on the VAT Return. This extra seven days also applies to paying HMRC so that the amount has cleared to HMRC's bank account. However this does not apply in these exceptional cases:

- The business uses the Annual Accounting Scheme for VAT

- The business is required to make payments on account (unless it submits monthly returns)

If the business pays HMRC by online Direct Debit, HMRC automatically collects payment from the bank account three bank working days after the extra seven calendar days following the normal due date.

If the business does not manage to pay cleared funds into HMRC's bank account by the payment deadline, or fails to have sufficient funds in its account to meet the direct debit, it may be liable to a surcharge for late payment.

Repayment of VAT

If the amount of VAT reclaimed (entered in Box 4) is more than the VAT to be paid (entered in Box 3), then the net VAT value in Box 5 is a repayment due to the business from HMRC.

HMRC is obliged to schedule this sum for repayment automatically, provided checks applied to the VAT Return do not indicate that such a repayment might not be due. There may be circumstances when the business does not receive the repayment automatically, for instance if there is an outstanding debt owed to HMRC.

SPECIAL ACCOUNTING SCHEMES

Annual Accounting Scheme for VAT

Using standard VAT accounting, four VAT Returns each year are required. Any VAT due is payable quarterly, and any VAT refunds due are also receivable quarterly.

Using annual VAT accounting, the business usually makes nine interim payments at monthly intervals. There is only one VAT Return to complete, at the end of the year, when either a balancing payment is made or it receives a balancing refund.

Businesses can use the annual accounting scheme if their estimated taxable turnover during the next tax year is not more than £1.35 million. Businesses already using the annual accounting scheme can continue to do so until the estimated taxable turnover for the next tax year exceeds £1.6 million.

Whilst using the annual accounting scheme the business may also be able to use either the cash accounting scheme or the flat rate scheme (but not both).

Benefits of annual accounting

- One VAT Return per year, instead of four.

- Two months after the tax period end to complete and send in the annual VAT return and pay the balance of VAT payable, rather than the usual one month.

- Better management of cash flow by paying a fixed amount in nine instalments.

- Ability to make additional payments as and when required.

- Join from VAT registration day, or at any other time if already registered.

Disadvantages of annual accounting

- Only one repayment per year, which is not beneficial if the business regularly requires refunds.

- If turnover decreases, interim payments may be higher than the VAT payments would be under standard VAT accounting – again there is a need to wait until the end of the year to receive a refund.

Cash Accounting Scheme for VAT

Using standard VAT accounting, VAT is paid on sales within a VAT period whether or not the customer has paid. Using cash accounting, VAT is not paid until the customer has paid the invoice. If a customer never pays, the business never has to pay the VAT.

Cash accounting can be used if the estimated taxable turnover during the next tax year is not more than £1.35 million. A business can continue to use cash accounting until its taxable turnover exceeds £1.6 million.

The cash accounting scheme may be used in conjunction with the annual accounting scheme.

Benefits of cash accounting

Using cash accounting may help cash flow, especially if customers are slow payers. Payment of VAT is not made until the business has received payment from the customer, so if a customer never pays, VAT does not have to be paid on that bad debt as long as the business is using the cash accounting scheme.

Disadvantages of cash accounting

Using cash accounting may adversely affect cash flow:

- The business cannot reclaim VAT on purchases until it has paid for them. This can be a disadvantage if most goods and services are purchased on credit.

- Businesses which regularly reclaim more VAT than they pay will usually receive repayment later under cash accounting than under standard VAT accounting, unless they pay for everything at the time of purchase.

- If a business starts using cash accounting when it starts trading, it will not be able to reclaim VAT on most start-up expenditure, such as initial stock, tools or machinery, until it has actually paid for those items.

- When it leaves the cash accounting scheme the business will have to account for all outstanding VAT due, including on any bad debts.

Flat Rate Schemes for VAT

If its VAT-exclusive taxable turnover is less than £150,000 per year, the business could simplify its VAT accounting by registering on the Flat Rate Scheme and calculating VAT payments as a percentage of its total VAT-inclusive turnover. There is no reclaim of VAT on purchases – this is taken into account in calculating the flat rate percentage that applies to the business. The flat rate scheme can reduce the time needed in accounting for and working out VAT. Even though the business still needs to show a VAT amount on each sales invoice, it does not need to record how much VAT it charged on every sale in its accounts. Nor does it need to record the VAT paid on every purchase.

Once on the scheme, the business can continue to use it until its total business income exceeds £230,000. The flat rate scheme may be used in conjunction with the annual accounting scheme.

Benefits of using a flat rate scheme

Using the flat rate scheme can save time and smooth cash flow. It offers these benefits:

- No need to record the VAT charged on every sale and purchase, as with standard VAT accounting. This can save time. There is no need to show VAT separately on invoices, as applies to standard VAT accounting.

- A first year discount. A business in its first year of VAT registration gets a 1% reduction in the applicable flat rate percentage until the day before the first anniversary of VAT registration.

- Fewer rules to follow, for instance no longer having to work out what VAT, on purchases, can or cannot be reclaimed.

- Peace of mind. With less chance of mistakes, there are fewer worries about getting the VAT right.

- Certainty. The business always knows what percentage of takings has to be paid to HMRC.

Potential disadvantages of using a flat rate scheme

The flat rate percentages are calculated in a way that takes into account zero-rated and exempt sales. They also contain an allowance for the VAT spent on purchases. So the VAT Flat Rate Scheme might not be right for the business if:

- it buys mostly standard-rated items, as there is no reclaim of any VAT on purchases

- it regularly receives a VAT repayment under standard VAT accounting

- it makes a lot of zero-rated or exempt sales

ERRORS

Action to be taken at the end of the VAT period

At the end of the VAT period, the business should calculate the net value of all the errors found during the period that relate to returns already submitted – that is, any tax which should have been claimed back is subtracted from any additional tax due to HMRC. Any deliberate errors must not be included – these must be separately disclosed to HMRC.

What the business should do next depends on whether the net value of all the errors is less than or greater than the 'error correction reporting threshold', which is the greater of:

- £10,000

- 1% of the box 6 figure on the VAT Return for the period when the error was discovered – subject to an upper limit of £50,000

If the net value of all the errors is less than the error reporting threshold then, if preferred, the errors may be corrected by making an adjustment on the current VAT Return (Method 1).

However, if the value of the net VAT error discovered is above this threshold, it must be reported to HMRC separately, in writing (Method 2).

How to adjust the VAT Return: Method 1

Errors from previous VAT returns can be corrected by adjusting the current VAT Return if the net value is below the error correction reporting threshold.

At the end of the VAT period when the errors are discovered, the VAT account of output tax due or input tax claimed is adjusted by the net amount of all errors. The VAT account must show the amount of the adjustment being made to the VAT Return.

If more than one error is discovered in the same exercise, the net value of all the errors is used to adjust the return.

Either box 1 or box 4 is adjusted, as appropriate. For example, if the business discovers that it didn't account for VAT payable to HMRC of £100 on a supply made in the past, and also didn't account for £60 VAT reclaimable on a purchase, it should add £40 to the box 1 figure on the current VAT return.

How to separately report an error to HMRC: Method 2

For certain errors a separate report is required to the relevant HMRC VAT Error Correction Team in writing about the mistake. The simplest way to tell them is to use Form VAT 652 "Notification of Errors in VAT Returns", which is for reporting errors on previous returns, but the business does not have to use Form VAT 652 – it can simply write a letter instead.

Businesses may, if they wish, use this method for errors of any size, even those which are below the error reporting threshold ie instead of a Method 1 error correction. Using this method means the business must not make adjustment for the same errors on a later VAT return.

Method 2 must always be used if the net errors exceed the error reporting threshold or if the errors made on previous returns were made deliberately.

SURCHARGES, PENALTIES AND ASSESSMENTS

Surcharges for missed VAT Return or VAT payment deadlines

VAT registered businesses must submit a VAT Return and pay any VAT by the relevant due date. If HMRC receives a return or VAT payment after the due date, the business is 'in default' and may have to pay a surcharge in addition to the VAT that is owed.

The first default is dealt with by a warning known as a 'Surcharge Liability Notice'. This notice tells the business that if it submits or pays late ('defaults') again during the following 12 months – known as the surcharge period – it may be charged a surcharge.

Submitting or paying late again during the surcharge period could result in a 'default surcharge'. This is a percentage of any unpaid VAT owed. Where a correct return is not submitted, HMRC will estimate the amount of VAT owed and base the surcharge on that amount (this is known as an assessment – see below).

HMRC assessments

Businesses have a legal obligation to submit VAT Returns and pay any VAT owed to HMRC by the relevant due date. If they don't submit a return, HMRC can issue an assessment which shows the amount of VAT that HMRC believes it is owed, based on their best estimate.

Penalties for careless and deliberate errors

Careless and deliberate errors will be liable to a penalty, whether they are adjusted on the VAT return or separately reported.

If a business discovers an error which is neither careless nor deliberate, HMRC expects that it will take steps to correct it. If the business fails to take steps to correct it, the inaccuracy will be treated as careless and a penalty will be due.

Penalties for inaccurate returns

Penalties may be applied if a VAT Return is inaccurate, and correcting this means tax is unpaid, understated, over-claimed or under-assessed. Telling HMRC about inaccuracies as soon as the business is aware of them may reduce any penalty that is due, in some cases to zero.

Penalty for late registration

Failure to register for VAT with HMRC at the right time may make a business liable to a late registration penalty.

FINDING OUT MORE INFORMATION ABOUT VAT

Most questions can be answered by referring to the HMRC website.

VAT Helpline

If the answer to a question is not on the HMRC website, the quickest and easiest way is to ring the VAT Helpline where most VAT questions can be answered.

Letters to HMRC

The VAT Helpline can answer most questions relating to VAT, but there may be times when it is more appropriate to write to HMRC.

This would apply if:

- the VAT information published by HMRC – either on the website or in printed notices and information sheets – has not answered a question

- the VAT Helpline has asked the business to write

- there is real doubt about how VAT affects a particular transaction, personal situation or business

If HMRC already publishes information that answers the question, their response will give the relevant details.

VISITS BY VAT OFFICERS

VAT officers are responsible for the collection of VAT for the government. They check businesses to make sure that their VAT records are up to date. They also check that amounts claimed from or paid to the government are correct. They examine VAT records, question the business owner or the person responsible for the VAT records and watch business activity.

Before a visit, HMRC will confirm the following details with the business:

- the person the VAT officer wants to see

- a mutually convenient appointment date and time

- the name and contact number of the officer carrying out the visit

- which records the officer will need to see, and for which tax periods

- how long the visit is likely to take

- any matters the business may be unsure of, so that the officer can be better prepared to answer queries

HMRC will confirm all the above information in writing with the business unless the time before the visit is too short to allow it. They will almost always give seven days notice of any visit unless an earlier one is more appropriate, for example to get a repayment claim paid more quickly.

Index

for your notes

for your notes